Eat Smart
IN
NORWAY

D0880324

Eat Smart IN NORWAY

**How to Decipher the Menu
Know the Market Foods
&
Embark on a Tasting Adventure**

Joan Peterson

GINKGO PRESS INC

Madison, Wisconsin

Eat Smart in Norway
Joan Peterson

Although the author and publisher have exhaustively researched all sources to ensure the accuracy and completeness of the information contained in this book, we assume no responsibility for errors, inaccuracies, omissions or any inconsistency herein. Any slights of people or organizations are unintentional.

Map lettering is by Gail L. Carlson; cover and insert photographs are by Joan Peterson; author photograph is by Susan Chwae.

The quote by James A. Michener from "This Great Big Wonderful World," from the March 1956 issue of Travel-Holiday Magazine, © 1956 by James A. Michener, is reprinted by permission of William Morris Endeavor Entertainment on behalf of the author.

Publisher's Cataloging-in-Publication
(Provided by Quality Books Inc.)
Peterson, Joan
   Eat smart in Norway : how to decipher the menu, know
the market foods & embark on a tasting adventure / Joan
Peterson
   p. cm.
   Includes bibliographical references and index.
   LCCN: 2010935627
   ISBN-13: 978-0-9776801-3-9
   ISBN-10: 0-9776801-3-4

   1. Cooking, Norwegian. 2. Diet--Norway. 3. Food
habits--Norway. 4. Cooking--Norway. 5. Norway--
Guidebooks. I. Title.

TX722.N6P48 2011   641.59481
                    QBI11-600117

Printed in the United States of America

To Svein and Anne-Grethe Aanestad

and, especially,

my Norwegian-American husband, David

Contents

through home visits to gain a deeper understanding of the
country, including its cuisine.

Helpful Phrases   79

Phrases in English translated to Norwegian, with additional
phonetic interpretation, which will assist you in finding,
ordering, and buying foods or ingredients.

Menu Guide   83

An extensive listing of menu entries in Norwegian, with English
translations, to make ordering food an easy and immediately
rewarding experience.

Foods and Flavors Guide   111

A comprehensive glossary of ingredients, kitchen utensils,
and cooking methods in Norwegian, with English translations.

Food Establishments   137

A quick reference guide to restaurants visited.

Preface

If you reject the food, ignore the customs, fear the religion and avoid the people, you might better stay home. You are like a pebble thrown into water; you become wet on the surface but you are never a part of the water.

—JAMES A. MICHENER

The publication of *Eat Smart in Norway* marks a milestone. It is the tenth EAT SMART guidebook I have written, either as sole author or in collaboration with another. Ginkgo Press also has begun to publish EAT SMART guides written solely by others. The first of these, *Eat Smart in France,* was penned by journalist and poet Ronnie Hess, whose background in French culture and experience with French cooking made her particularly well-suited to tackle the topic of French cuisine.

The purpose of the EAT SMART guides is to provide information for travelers that will empower and encourage them to sample new and often unusual foods, and will allow them to discover new ways of preparing or combining familiar ingredients. I know travelers will be more open to experimentation when they are informed. The EAT SMART guides also will help steer travelers away from the foods they wish to avoid—very few people truly enjoy all foods!

This guide (like others in the series) has four main chapters. The first provides an encapsulated history of Norwegian cuisine; the second gives an overview of the modern cuisine and describes regional differences and specialties. Other main chapters provide extensive menu listings and a glossary of terms associated with the preparation and serving of food, arranged alphabetically, and placed at the back of the book for easy reference.

National favorites, regional classics, and personal picks are designated by marginal comments. Do try to sample as many of them as you can.

The book also includes practical information for travelers, including phrases that will be useful in markets, shops, and restaurants. There is a chapter of recipes provided by Norwegian chefs and home cooks, all taste-tested in the EAT SMART kitchens. Perhaps you would enjoy preparing some of the dishes as a preview of Norwegian food before your travels, or as a remembrance of your visit when you return home. Because there are more than four million people of Norwegian descent in the United States, most ingredients in the recipes can be readily obtained here. Substitutions for unavailable ingredients are given. Sources for Norwegian foodstuffs can be found in the *Resources* chapter, which also cites groups that offer the opportunity to have person-to-person contact through home visits to gain a deeper understanding of the country and its cuisine.

JOAN PETERSON
Madison, Wisconsin

Acknowledgments

I gratefully acknowledge those who assisted me in making this book possible. Thanks to Gail Carlson for enlivening the maps with her handwriting; Susan Chwae for the cover design, author photograph, and pre-publication technical assistance; Nicol Knappen (Ekeby) for book design; and Todd Michelson-Ambelang and Anna Rue (University of Wisconsin graduate program in the Department of Scandinavian Studies), author Nils Harald Moe (Tromsø), Marit Renslemo (Nesbyen), and Per Sverre Øvrum (Skien) for assistance with translation.

For contributing recipes (regrettably, some could not be used because of space limitations) and/or providing cooking demonstrations, I thank the following chefs, food and wine professionals, cookbook authors, and "home cooks": Anne-Grethe Aanestad (Heddel); Nils Averå (Fleischer's Hotel, Voss); Maria Berglind (Fretheim Hotel, Flåm); Randi Engelsen Eide, Aud Walaker Hutchinson, Valborg Kløve-Graue, Renate Lunde, and Eli Skjervheim (The Vossahuldrene, Voss); Mikael Forselius (Røros Hotell, Røros); Hanne Frosta (Hanne på Høyden, Bergen); Heine Grov (freelance chef, Byrne); Bjorg Harman (Gransherad); Ole-Erik Holmen-Løkken (To Rom og Kjokken, Trondheim); Kristoffer Hovland and Ståle Johansen (Fossheim Hotell, Lom); Kirsti Indreeide (Petrines Gjestgiveri, Norddal); Inge Johnsen (Sans & Samling Lian Restaurant, Trondheim); Walter Kieliger (Frognerseteren, Oslo); Daniel Olsen (Enhjørningen Fiskerestaurant, Bergen); Robert Ottesen (Sjohuset Skagen, Stavanger); Morten Rathe (Rica Nidelven Hotel, Trondheim); Knut Renslemo (Nesbyen); Eric Saudan (Bryggen Tracteursted, Bergen); Frode Selvaag (Spa-Hotell Velvære, Hjelmeland); Gro Sevle (Sevletunet, Nore og Uvdal); Geir Skeie (Brygga 11, Sandefjord); Anna Solheim and Randi Øvstebø (Byrkjedalstunet, Dirdal); Gunhild Vevik (Region Stavanger BA); and Per Sverre Øvrum (Skien).

ACKNOWLEDGMENTS

Others who gave freely of their time to explain the nuances of Norwegian food and food history were: Anne-Grethe and Svein Aanestad (Heddel); author and chef Arne Brimi (Brimiland); chef Mikael Forselius (Røros Hotell, Røros); Ejdre Gabrielsen and Anders Hellegaard, food and beverage consultant and director, respectively (Culinary Institute of Norway, Stavanger); author and chef Scott Givot (past president, International Association of Culinary Professionals, Oslo); author Ingrid Espelid Hovig (Oslo); chef Inge Johnsen (Sans & Samling Lian Restaurant, Trondheim); author Lisa Laa (Laa Gjestestugu, Ål); author Nils Harald Moe (Tromsø); chef Knut Renslemo and Marit Renslemo (Nesbyen); author Astri Riddervold (Oslo); Eric Saudan (owner, Bryggen Tracteursted, Bergen); Thor Bull Skarvatun (Sterling White Halibut AS); Monika Sunde (Byrkjedalstunet, Dirdal); Andreas and Edith Søli (Skien); Leif Inge Underdal and Ivar-Bjarne Underdal (Undredal Stølsysteri and Norsk Gardsost); Gunhild Vevik (Region Stavanger BA); and Per Sverre Øvrum (Skien).

Special thanks also to those who shared useful contacts and information: Anne Arnesen; Marie Bakås (Form til Fjells, Røros); Andrea Christofferson and Raphael Kadushin (University of Wisconsin Press); Lisbeth Fallan (VisitTrondheim AS); Virginia Goeke; Jon Grinde; Harald Hansen (Innovations Norway); Lauritz Hansen and Frode Idsøe (Skagen Brygge Hotell, Stavanger); Robert Hughes; Astrid Klove-Graue (Avisa Hordaland, Voss); Thomas Loftus (former United States Ambassador to Norway); Bill Lubing; Trygve Lønnebotn (former Wisconsin Honorary Consul for Norway); Kristine Marion; David L. Nelson, MD; David Peterson; chef Knut Renslemo (Nesbyen); and Jason Sederquist.

Thanks also to Beate Andersen and Ingerid Lund (*News of Norway* magazine); Hilde Grotnes Arnesen (The Hanseatic Museum, Bergen); Siv Falk (National Historical Museum, Stockholm); Linn Kjos Falkenberg (Bergen Tourist Board); Tom Gustavsen; Elvind Heiberg (CEO, Sons of Norway); Peter Kaland (University of Bergen); Sigrid Kaland (University of Bergen Museum); Elin Kvamme (Slow Food, Bergen); Trond Lødøen (University of Bergen); Kjersten Moody and Carrie Roy (University of Wisconsin graduate program in the Department of Scandinavian Studies); food and travel journalist Marie Peyre; and Jason Sederquist.

And special thanks to Brook Soltvedt, good friend and editor extraordinaire.

Map of Norway

The Cuisine of Norway

An Historical Survey

Situated at the northern tip of Europe, Norway is a long and narrow expanse of land with a bulge at each end. The mainland—extending from about 57 degrees north to 71 degrees north—lies on the western edge of the Scandinavian Peninsula, a land mass comprising the countries of Norway, Sweden, and a small strip of northern Finland. The country shares a long eastern border with Sweden and a shorter, northeastern border with Finland. In the far north, the land curves over Finland and abuts the border of the Russian Federation. Norway's western boundaries are the Norwegian and North Seas.

The Scandinavian Mountains, which the Norwegians call Kjølen (keel), form the backbone of the peninsula. This range is skewed toward the western edge of the peninsula, so the mountains are principally in Norway in the south. In the narrower, northern reaches of Norway, the mountains form the border between Norway and Sweden, and in the northeast, they veer towards Finland. The western side of the mountains drops abruptly to the sea. Glaciers long ago etched deep valleys into the mountains, and seawater filled many of them after the ice melted, forming the dramatic and exquisitely beautiful fjords. The gently sloping eastern flank of the range is in Sweden.

Norway's coastline is extremely long and jagged. Including the fjords and minor indentations, its length is about 15,500 miles. Add to that the coastlines of the islands and the rocky points or reefs (skerries) sheltering the shore—approximately 50,000 of them—and the length increases several-fold to about 52,000 miles.

While the Norwegian landscape is incredibly beautiful, the environment is harsh, necessitating adaptation to its limitations. Forests blanket close to 40 percent of the country and two thirds of the terrain is mountainous, with a little over 30 percent above the tree line. Most of the country is snow-covered for more than 6 months of the year, and close to half lies above the Arctic

Circle. Yet, the climate is less severe than would be expected at such high latitudes because the warm Atlantic currents—the Gulf Stream and its continuation, the North Atlantic Current—moderate the climate along the coast. Not surprisingly then, a mere 3 percent of the land is suitable for agriculture, in pockets along the coast and in certain mountain and lowland valleys.

Geography generally determines areas suitable for habitation, so it is not surprising that the nation is unevenly and sparsely populated: some 5 million people live in Norway at a density of 34 per square mile. Forty percent of Norwegians live in the area surrounding the Oslofjord, which includes Oslo, the nation's capitol situated at the apex of the fjord.

Until the 20th century, Norway had not been occupied by outside forces by virtue of its relative isolation from the European countries farther south and its inhospitable terrain. While this has spared Norway a multitude of tragedies, it also has, over the centuries, minimized exposure to new foods and to the cooking influences of other cultures. These would have to come to Norway via the sea trade.

Early Beginnings

Practically all of the ice cap covering Norway in the last Ice Age had melted by 7000 BCE. Tundra-like vegetation emerged, providing favorable grazing for herds of reindeer that later would tempt arctic hunters.

The first migrations of people into Norway came mainly from the south. Southern Sweden at that time was connected to Denmark, and hence to the European Continent, by a land bridge that existed because sea levels were low and most of the North Sea was dry. Small, scattered groups of people from the continent presumably made their way north along this bridge to Sweden and then into southern Norway. Evidence of human habitation in Norway from these first migrations has been found along the southeastern coast, east of the Oslofjord, and along the western coast as far north as central Norway. The implements found in the settlements indicate that this culture (Fosna) hunted and fished in the coastal regions and hunted reindeer in the mountains.

Traces of human life were also found at Komsa in Finnmark on the northern coast of Norway. The Komsa culture of hunters and fishermen apparently was entirely coastal, and may have entered northeastern Norway from Finland or Russia in the vicinity of the Varanger Peninsula. According

2

to some archaeologists, the indigenous arctic culture in northern Norway known as the Sámi or Lapps may be descended from the Komsa culture.

The first farming society, the Early Funnel Beaker Culture, appeared in the vicinity of the Oslofjord in southeastern Norway in the Early Neolithic Period, 4000–3300 BCE. The vegetation of this area and the specific crops that the early agriculturalists grew have been deduced from an analysis of pollen found in bogs and in lake-bottom sediment. The land was covered with dense forests of oak, elm, lime, and ash, which were cleared with axes and by fire to provide land for planting barley and growing pastoral crops of plantain, nettle, and wormwood (fat hen). Goats and sheep were domesticated. Agriculture and animal husbandry were also in evidence at this time in a few areas along the southern and western coasts.

There have been conflicting views concerning the origin of the first Norwegian farmers. Archeologists initially determined that they migrated from continental Europe. Current consensus holds that hunter-gatherer cultures already in Norway began to adopt agriculture as a result of a dramatic climate change that caused drier and warmer conditions more favorable for farming. Foraging, hunting, and fishing remained important.

The pottery vessels crafted by the first farmers had flared tops and round bottoms, decorated with vertical impressions made by imprinting wet clay with cording, or by scraping it with a comb. This pottery style was called funnel beaker, and it served to identify the culture.

Agriculturists known as the Battle-Axe / Corded Ware Culture date from the Middle Neolithic Period B, 2800–2400 BCE. Their culture was named for its polished stone battle-axe, which had a characteristic hole for shafting, and for its pottery, which was decorated by imprinting wet clay with twisted cording. This elaboration of the Funnel Beaker Culture's style of decorating pottery indicates close contact between the two cultures, which also employed similar agricultural practices.

Funnel beaker, a round-bottomed vessel with flared top, characteristic of the Funnel Beaker Culture in Early and Middle Neolithic Scandinavia (4000–2800 BCE). National Historical Museum, Stockholm. Reprinted with permission.

3

The Battle-Axe / Corded Ware Culture had settlements along the southern coast and as far north as central Norway on the western coast.

By the Late Neolithic Period, 2400–1700 BCE, agriculture and animal husbandry became the dominant economy. Agriculture spread farther inland, into the high mountain plateaus and into northern Norway. Fields were cultivated with a primitive plow (ard), a horizontal wooden frame with a hoe-like vertical blade attached to one end, which simply loosened the soil. Rock art paintings show that the ard was drawn by oxen. Carts were drawn by horses.

The earliest fossilized grains have been found in coastal settlements as far north as central Norway. They include naked barley (without hulls) and the earliest cultivated forms of wheat: emmer, einkorn, and spelt. Bones from sheep, goats, and a smaller number of cattle have also been found at these settlements.

The archaeological record indicates that at this time agrarian farmsteads began to have dwellings large enough for several households. These habitations, known as longhouses, were up to 75 feet long, and each may have provided shelter for as many as 30 people. Longhouses were constructed with one or two lengthwise rows of posts down the middle to support the roof, effectively dividing the houses into three longitudinal aisles. The walls typically consisted of a woven lattice of wooden strips (wattle) spread with a sticky plaster (daub), a mixture of wet dirt, manure, and straw.

Trading with other cultures was evident at this time. Late Neolithic peoples built boats sturdy enough to cross the Strait of Skagerrak to the southwestern coast of Sweden and to the Jutland peninsula of Denmark. Danish flintsmiths made remarkable and technologically complex parallel-flaked flint daggers and tools. Their crescent-shaped sickle blades were strapped to wooden handles and used to harvest grain. Secondary products from domestic and wild animals—milk, hides, horns, bones, wool, fur, and manure—became valuable commodities that Norwegians could exchange for flint and amber. Thus trade became important to the economic welfare of Norwegian settlements.

During the Bronze Age, 1700–500 BCE, tools and weapons were made of bronze, an alloy of copper and tin. Although these metals were not found in Norway, local metalsmiths became proficient at smelting and casting bronze pieces from imported ores. Their products augmented the assortment of coveted bronze articles that trickled into Norway through trade.

The number of agrarian farmsteads increased significantly in this period, with corresponding deforestation in regions where farmsteads were densely concentrated. Farmers understood that soil enriched with manure yielded healthier crops. Hulled barley, which thrives in enriched soil, became more important than naked barley in the Late Bronze Age, and flax, a new crop, was grown for its seeds and fibers. Little emmer or spelt wheat was cultivated at the time. Although the technology to make bronze tools was now available, sickles with flint blades were still used to harvest grain. Only a single bronze sickle dating to this period has been found.

Bone deposits from the Bronze Age indicate that domestic pigs were being raised in addition to sheep, goats, and cattle. Cattle barns came into existence. Longhouses were constructed with a barn and living quarters at opposite ends, separated by an entryway in the middle. The barns were used for storing fodder. The smaller longhouses of the time suggest single-family dwellings, and that the livestock within was privately owned. In some instances, stone fences enclosed cultivated fields, a sign of developing individual property rights.

Exceptional rock carvings from this period depict many scenes connected with farming, fishing, and boating. Early artists painted their carvings with red ochre, a pigmented clay.

The transition to the Iron Age took place around 500 BCE. The gradual deterioration of the climate that occurred at the beginning of the Pre-Roman phase of the Iron Age (500 BCE – 1) was a challenging time for agriculture. The weather became colder and wetter, conditions that favored the growth of certain grains over others. Hulled barley did well, as did oats and rye, which were introduced during this time. In the first known written account of Norway by a foreign visitor (330 BCE), Pytheas, a Greek explorer and

Bronze Age rock art carving depicting a two-wheeled cart drawn by two horses, with a human figure riding on the cart. The carving is located at Unneset V, Askvoll, Sogn og Fjordane county in western Norway. Tracing provided by Trond Lødøen, University of Bergen.

5

geographer from present-day Marseilles, recorded that the people he encountered on the western shore of Norway above the Arctic Circle ate oats, vegetables, roots, and wild fruit.

Both the population and the size of settlements increased during the Iron Age. There were villages or hamlets comprised of many farms clustered together, with each farm having its own plot of land outside the village.

Articles of iron—sickles, knives, awls, spears, jewelry, and belt buckles—initially were forged from small amounts of the metal present in some of the copper ores used to make bronze. Later, iron-bearing bogs became the main source of raw material.

Farms in the Roman phase of the Iron Age (1–400) had all the key farm buildings and patterns of land usage that have been retained up to the present: dwellings for people and livestock, fenced fields in close proximity to the buildings, and a path for herding cattle from the barn to fenced pastures in the outlying area. Longhouses sheltered man and beast under one roof, but the barn and house compartments were partitioned into several rooms. Smaller buildings were used for metal work, storage, and crafts.

Oats, barley, and flax continued to play a key role in the diet. Oats were typical fare, usually eaten as porridge. Barley was more common inland and in the north, and was the basis for beer and mead. With the invention of rotating querns, milling flour became more efficient.

The Migration phase (400–600) was a time of upheaval throughout Europe as combat escalated between the Western Roman Empire and various northern Germanic tribes. As the Empire lost strength (finally collapsing in 476), Germanic tribes, driven by population pressure and frequent invasions by the fierce, nomadic Huns, migrated throughout Europe, seeking new land. Some Germanic peoples migrated to the coastal region of western Norway. The Ryger and Horder tribes settled there in the fifth century and contributed their names to modern-day Rogaland and Hordaland counties.

The last phase of the Iron Age (600–800) is called the Merovingian phase because strong influences from Frankish Merovingian culture can be seen in weaponry, dress, ornaments, and household objects found as grave artifacts from this time.

Archeological records indicate that there was little change in the grain diet—cultivated crops consisted of wheat, rye, barley, oats, and flax. Owing to the climate, relatively little barley was grown in arctic Norway. The food consumed there included fish and sea mammals, birds and bird eggs, meat, and milk. Reindeer were the primary source of meat for the indigenous Sámi.

The Vikings

Population growth and increased opportunities for piracy were instrumental in setting the stage for raids by the pagan "Norsemen," the Vikings. Shipbuilding at the beginning of the Viking Age (800–1100) had become relatively sophisticated. The dreaded Viking longboats had keels for stability and sails for speed, making seafaring, exploration, and piracy possible over greater distances. Initially the Vikings sought plunder—precious metals, gems, and slaves—and later, land. Their expeditions took them both eastward and westward. Some founded colonies and never returned home nor took to the high seas again. The Viking period officially begins with a raid in England in 789, duly recorded in the *Anglo-Saxon Chronicle*. Thus both written documentation and the archaeological record provide insight into the history and culture of the Viking period, which lasted about 300 years, until 1066.

During the Viking period wealthy farmers no longer shared their longhouses with livestock. The living area of a longhouse had dual-purpose platforms for sitting and sleeping, which ran along both long walls. Meals were prepared in the center of the living area over an elevated open hearth lined with flat, upright stones. Iron-handled cooking pots made of welded metal plates or carved of soapstone were hung over the hearth from a tripod by means of an adjustable hook that allowed the pots to be raised or lowered over the fire. Pots also were suspended over the hearth by iron chains attached to the ceiling beams. Town dwellings included additional space for workshops and businesses.

There were two principal meals per day, one in the morning and one in the evening. Knives were used to cut meat, spoons to eat porridge. But most food was eaten with the fingers. Dishware and cooking utensils were primarily made of wood and included round plates (trenchers), small rectangular troughs for porridges, and bowls for milk. Other beverages were drunk out of vessels made from ox horns. Butter churns, storage barrels, large troughs for kneading dough, and a collection of vessels used for the various processes of brewing beer were made of wood.

A considerable variety of foods was available in the Viking Age, and at least the wealthy ate well. Cattle were the main source of meat, although lamb, goat, venison, pork, and poultry were also consumed, either boiled or spit-roasted. Meat was dried, salted, or smoked to preserve it. Cod, as well as freshwater salmon and perch, were the main fish eaten. Vegetables in the diet were beans, peas, carrots, onions, wild leeks, garlic, and edible seaweed.

Vikings returned home from the British Isles with turnips and cabbage. Several kinds of wild fruit and berries were enjoyed, including apples, plums, pears, strawberries, blueberries, and cloudberries. Wild hazelnuts were also eaten. Thin, unleavened flatbread was made from barley, oat, or rye flour. The dough was kneaded in rectangular wooden troughs and baked over the fire on long-handled iron pans. Flavors were enhanced with garlic, leeks, mustard, horseradish, cumin, and herbs, notably angelica (*Angelica archangelica*), which has a juniper-like flavor. Honey was used a sweetener, and salt was obtained by boiling seawater. Milk and whey were enjoyed as beverages, but milk was also made into butter and cheese. The Vikings brewed beer from malted barley and hops, made wine from fermented fruit juices, and made mead from a boiled and fermented mixture of honey and water.

Dried fish, primarily cod, was a vital commodity for seafaring Vikings, both for sustenance and for trade. In the ninth century the Basques in northern Spain, who were experienced in salt-curing whale meat, showed the Vikings how to extend the shelf life of dried fish by salting it first. The cod industry would become big business in the centuries ahead.

Crop rotation was practiced at the beginning of the Viking Age. Rye was sown in the fall, followed by barley and oats in the summer. Later the field was manured or fertilized with humus, seaweed, algae, or fish offal, and allowed to lie fallow for a year. Wheat was sown where growing conditions were suitable. But the Vikings often relied on imported wheat to augment supplies.

Some of the early Norwegian Vikings ventured eastward through Russia. Along the way, they obtained slaves and furs that they traded for silver. They ultimately reached Constantinople (now Istanbul) but were unable to conquer the city. Many remained and served the Byzantine emperors as elite bodyguards, forming the foreign mercenary group called the Varangian Guard. Those who returned home from Constantinople brought valuable commodities including previously unknown spices—cardamom, ginger, nutmeg, and pepper. Cardamom, especially, has remained a favorite spice in Norwegian baking.

At the close of the Viking Age, Norway's many communities became unified. The consolidation began in 872 with the defeat of powerful northern chieftains by King Harald Hårfagre (Harald Fairhair) near present-day Stavanger in western Norway. By 1060, all of modern Norway was united under a single king, King Harald Sigurdsson. The Viking's last gasp came when King Harald invaded England in 1066. He was defeated and killed at the Battle of Stamford Bridge by King Harold Godwinson of England and his forces.

Replica of a Viking-Age long-handled iron griddle, about 10 inches in diameter, with slightly raised edges, used to bake flatbread in a clay oven or over an open hearth. From the collection of Astri Riddervold, Oslo. Photographed with permission.

Medieval Norway

The codfish industry underwent a significant change in the Medieval Age (1066–1520). Christianity had spread into Norway during the Viking Age, and the Catholic practice of religious fasting, which proscribed eating meat on holy days, made dried cod a key export commodity. What had been a trading enterprise to acquire luxury goods and garner prestige, now became big business.

At the start of the twelfth century, large-scale fishing activities focused on the Lofoten and Vesterålen archipelagos above the Arctic Circle. After January, the arctic cod in the Barents Sea (called *skrei* in their spawning stage) migrate about 500 miles to their spawning grounds near the archipelagos. Fish were caught through the end of March and air-dried.

The coastal city of Bergen in western Norway became the principal center for exportation of dried fish (mainly cod) and other goods, and for the importation of grain. Among the merchants doing business in Bergen, the Germans were early arrivals, buying fish and selling grain, flour, and malt. These merchants took up winter residence in Bergen, which helped position them for privileged trade status.

Bergen became one of the four most important cities in the Hanseatic League. This federation began as a partnership between merchants in the German towns of Lübeck and Hamburg in the mid-twelfth century; at its height it was a powerful multinational network of alliances of merchants from about 200 cities and towns throughout Europe. The League defended its members' vessels from piracy, negotiated free-trade agreements, and established trading posts where the League merchants lived and did business, often quite separate from the native population.

Bergen's port gained a virtual monopoly for transshipping dried cod from Norwegian fisheries in the north to the British Isles and northern continental Europe. Merchants with the Hanseatic League established permanent quarters at Bryggen (the wharf). This old commercial center along the eastern shore of the harbor remains today and is on UNESCO's list of World Heritage Sites. By the fourteenth century the Hanseatic League so dominated trade in Bergen that Norwegian merchants were virtually excluded.

In the late 1900s a study was conducted to determine the types of plant materials that were eaten during medieval times in three Norwegian cities— Bergen (western Norway), Trondheim (central Norway), and Oslo (eastern Norway). The towns had different relationships to the Hanseatic League: Bergen, an important branch of the League; Trondheim, no contact; and Oslo, a minor trading station. Archaeological excavations were made of refuse layers and latrine remains found beneath the areas inhabited during the Medieval Age. In Bergen, samples were taken from Bryggen, the old German settlement, and from the Norwegian residential area surrounding it. Additional information about the food was gleaned from written sources.

The general pattern to emerge from the samples obtained is that the Norwegians in the three towns primarily ate locally grown plants. There was a close relationship between what was eaten in town and what was cultivated or grew wild in the adjacent countryside. Among the produce were hazelnuts, sour cherries, apples, plums, pears, raspberries, cloudberries, black crowberries, strawberries, cabbage, peas, beans, and turnips. Herbs and spices included angelica (an herb in the parsley family), fennel, henbane, opium poppy, black mustard, and juniper. Dietary grains were oats, barley, and wheat. Barley was especially important because of its use in brewing beer. Imported malt was used in the process. The Germans in Bergen flavored their beer with hops, the Norwegians with sweet gale. The presence in the samples of figs, grapes, and walnuts, which are not indigenous to Norway, and rye, which was not an important crop in Norway at the time, was a measure of the foreign influence in the towns.

Monasteries were instrumental in the development and spread of fruit cultivation. During the Medieval Age more than thirty monasteries were founded in Norway, most of which were located along the southern and western coasts. English Cistercian monks established Lyse Monastery in 1146 in present-day Hardanger, a traditional district in western Norway known for its orchards. The cultivation of apples, plums, pears, and cherries in Hardanger originated with these monks.

Many farmhouses of the era had two floors. An enclosed hearth, or fireplace, was placed in one corner and was fitted with a chimney, which allowed the second floor to be heated. Farms often had a storage building, sometimes with a second-floor loft.

Much is known about the beverages available in Medieval Norway. The most common was milk, typically soured to extend its shelf life. Whey, too, was soured and drunk. Soured milk was used to make cheese. Alcoholic beverages were popular. Most beer was brewed locally; most wine and mead was imported.

The Black Death (bubonic plague) came to Norway in 1349. The epidemic, introduced to Bergen by rats and their plague-infested fleas in a grain shipment, spread rapidly through the country. It struck harder here than elsewhere in Europe and killed over half of the population. The country went through a severe crisis as the power of its institutions weakened. Many farms and villages were deserted. The population became primarily one of peasant farmers, with only about five percent of the peasants living in the few towns that existed during this time. In general, grain production fell and animal husbandry increased. The price of animal products rose, and land rents were often paid to land owners in butter (or in dried fish in the north), rather than grain. The most important connection between the Norwegian peasant economy and the world market at the time was through exportation of dried fish.

In 1380, Denmark and a weakened Norway were politically united through intermarriage between the ruling families. As a result of dynastic ties, Norway, Denmark, and Sweden entered into the Kalmar Union in 1397, which joined the three countries under a single monarch. Sweden declared its independence in 1524, ending the Kalmar Union, but Norway remained united with Denmark under the Oldenburg dynasty.

The Danish Era

The kings of the Oldenburg dynasty resided in Denmark; few set foot in Norway. Under Danish rule (1380–1814), Norway lost much of its social and economic connection with the rest of Europe. This period is often referred to as the 400-year night.

Norway's first dictionary, *Den Norske Dictionarium eller Glosebog* (The Norwegian Dictionary or Book of Words), proved to be an unexpected source of information about Norwegian cuisine at the time. It was compiled in 1646 by Christian Jenssøn, a pastor in the village of Askvoll, near his birthplace of Bergen. Along with about 900 entries pertaining to nature, history, and culture, there were recipes for some dishes prepared in his village. Several recipes were for making cheeses, such as the cheese called *rørost* made from soured milk, for which Henry Notaker provided a translation in *A Thousand Years of Norwegian Food:* "one takes one or more barrels of milk, and, before lighting the fire, stirs this frequently in a pan with the handle of a broom until it becomes as thin as fresh milk. The pan is then placed on a low fire, and heated until it is warmer than tepid, but not so warm that a hand cannot be immersed in it. When curdling occurs, one removes the curds, places a cloth of coarse, clean linen into a bowl, and places the curd into the cloth. A heavy object is then placed on top of the curds, such that all the whey is pressed out."

The dried codfish industry expanded to include a salted product. Centuries ago, the Vikings had learned from the Basques that salting fish prior to drying it preserved it longer than drying alone. The availability of salt, however, was limited. Norwegians produced salt by boiling or evaporating seawater, but the product was inferior and not easy to attain in sufficient quantity. It was not until the Hanseatic League took over the importation of salt to northern countries that the salt-cod industry could flourish in Norway on a large scale.

A Dutchman, Jappe Ippes, was granted royal privilege from the king of Denmark in 1691 to produce and export salted, dried cod. The fish were called *klippfisk* (cliff fish) because they were placed on rocky cliffs near the shore during the summer to dry in the sun and wind. Production of *klippfisk* began in the coastal town of Fosen, now called Kristiansund, in western Norway. Decapitated, butterflied fish were salted in Lofoten in northern Norway prior to being shipped to Fosen to be dried. Spanish seafarers who bought the fish in Kristiansund a couple of centuries later, in the 1800s, introduced their style of cooking salt cod, which became a classic dish of Kristiansund—*bacalao.*

The herring industry also benefitted from the availability of salt. Herring, an essential in the Norwegian diet since prehistoric times, was brined and smoked. It became *husmannskost,* or common food for people of limited means.

In 1740, northern Norway developed a vital trade relationship with the Pomor people of coastal northwest Russia. The Pomors shipped their

Decocting salt by boiling seawater that had been hoisted up from the depths of the sea in hollowed-out tree trunks. Woodcut by Olaus Magnus, 1555, *Description of the Northern Peoples,* Book Thirteen, Chapter 43.

goods—rye and wheat flour, oats, peas, meat, and dairy products—from the port town of Arkhangelsk to the town of Vardø in present-day Finnmark county, and traded them for fish. These shipments were especially crucial during the years when grain harvests failed.

The single, most revolutionary change in the Norwegian diet during this era was the introduction of the potato in the 1750s, probably from England or Scotland. The clergy, the first to advocate potato cultivation, grew the crop on farmland associated with their parsonages. The potato was a more reliable crop than grain and could be grown on land that supported the growth of little else. It profoundly affected the quality of life, lowering mortality rates and contributing to the rise in population. Until recently a dinner without boiled potatoes was almost unthinkable. Potatoes also replaced grain in the distillation of spirits.

Norway under Sweden

The union between Denmark and Norway was dissolved in 1814 after the Napoleonic Wars. Denmark, unlike Sweden, had supported the losing side in the Napoleonic wars, and Norway was ceded to Sweden by the provisions of the Peace Treaty of Kiel. Norway, resisting this new subordination, went ahead and framed a constitution, establishing itself as an independent country with a Danish king, Christian I. A brief war ensued, with Sweden emerging victorious. Christian was banished, but Norway's new constitution was acknowledged. Norway and Sweden remained united under a Swedish king, but as independent states with separate parliaments. The union lasted until 1905.

Agriculture changed profoundly in the latter half of the 1800s. Farming became more efficient with the production of new equipment, and the need for additional labor (crofters) on the farms was lessened. Dairy farm cooperatives formed when butter- and cheese-making on single farms was no longer profitable. There was a large exodus of people from rural areas to the towns, especially in southern Norway. Economic concerns and crop failures led to waves of emigration to America.

The Industrial Revolution also brought important improvements in the kitchen. The manufacture of cast-iron wood-burning stoves in Norway began in the early 1800s. With more than one cooking spot on the stovetop at their disposal, women could now cook several things simultaneously, and the traditional "one pot" open hearth or fireplace method of cooking gradually phased out.

The first printed cookbook in Norwegian appeared in 1831. It was geared to the expanding urban middle class now cooking on the new stoves. At first credited to several anonymous housewives, authorship was later attributed to Maren Elizabeth Bang. *Huusholdnings-Bog: indrettet efter den almindelige Brug i norske Huusholdninger* (Household Book: Arranged for Ordinary Use in Norwegian Households) included recipes and a guide to housekeeping. In 1845 Hanna Winsnes wrote what would become the classic Norwegian cookbook of the nineteenth century: *Lærebog i de Forskjellige Grene af Huusholdningen* (Textbook in the Different Subjects of the Household). It contained hundreds of recipes and provided advice on how to grow, buy, prepare, and preserve foods, as well how to slaughter and brew. She also discussed how to organize large rural households, information that was especially useful when workloads had to be adjusted to handle the seasonal demands of making cheese and other dairy products in the summer and slaughtering animals in the fall. Hanna Winsnes, a prolific writer, also produced a pamphlet entitled *For fattige Huusmødre* (For Poor Housewives) in 1857, in which she described how to utilize every part of an animal and how to get the most out of a small garden.

In the 1840s restaurants began to appear in Norway. They, like most of the cookbooks written at the time, catered primarily to the middle class.

14

From Independence to the Present

In 1905 the union with Sweden was dissolved. For the first time since the end of the Medieval Age, Norway was an independent nation. In a referendum, Norwegians chose a monarchy, offering the throne to a Danish prince. The mechanization of household chores made women's work easier. Milking machines, milk separators, and meat grinders were introduced. Ground meat no longer was a privilege of the wealthy because it no longer required servants to mince it with knives. Meatballs could now be enjoyed by anyone. The availability of baking ovens led to the production of leavened bread, especially loaves of rye and wheat.

After World War II the tradition of peasant farming ended. Most farms became independent single-household operations. Farmers' cooperatives assisted in achieving self-sufficiency in food production.

Norway experienced rapid economic growth. The discovery of large deposits of oil and gas in the North Sea led Norway to become a major oil and gas exporter in the mid-1970s.

With the rise of tourism in the 1960s, foreign culinary traditions were introduced. Shops in the large cities began to stock a wide selection of imported foods. Fast foods and fast food chains also pervaded the culinary scene. Frozen pizza represents an enormous commercial success story. Norway's own vastly popular brand, Grandiosa, has been produced since the 1980s. A gourmet restaurant culture inspired by French cuisine developed, followed by a more recent trend to apply continental techniques to traditional Norwegian ingredients.

For some, foreign culinary influences have gone too far. A group of chefs in the five Nordic countries began an effort in 2008 to staunch the influx of foreign cooking terms into the names of dishes on restaurant menus. Called New Nordic Food (*Ny Nordisk Mat*), the program's intent is to reinforce the identity of the Nordic kitchen on menus for foreign diners by describing dishes in the native Nordic language (with appropriate English translations, if given) to strengthen the feeling for the food's origins. There is also a back-to-our-roots movement calling for a return to traditional foods and the use of artisanal products.

Map of Norway

COUNTIES OF NORWAY

Eastern Norway
1. Østfold
2. Akershus
3. Oslo
4. Hedmark
5. Oppland
6. Buskerud
7. Vestfold
8. Telemark

Southern Norway
9. Aust-Agder
10. Vest-Agder

Western Norway
11. Rogaland
12. Hordaland
13. Sogn og Fjordane
14. Møre og Romsdal

Central Norway
15. Sør-Trøndelag
16. Nord-Trøndelag

Northern Norway
17. Nordland
18. Troms
19. Finnmark

Regional Norwegian Food

A Quick Tour of Norwegian Foods and Their Regional Variations

Norwegian Food in a Nutshell

The culinary ingenuity of the early Norwegians was remarkable. Less than 3 percent of the land was suitable for growing crops—in pockets along the coast and in certain mountain and lowland valleys—and only a limited variety of foodstuffs was produced during the short growing season. Despite the hardships dealt by nature and climatic conditions, these rugged people managed to sustain themselves through long winters by preserving the food they had grown or gathered, meat they had hunted or trapped, and fish they had harvested. They created many clever and resourceful dishes from these stored provisions.

Traditional Norwegian food is based on the simple fare of peasants. There was no aristocratic class to develop a culinary tradition as there had been in some other European countries. Staple foods were, and still are, fish, meat, dairy products, grains, root vegetables, and berries.

Fresh foods are relished in season. Traditional dishes tend to appear on the table when their signature ingredients are available. And even though most foods can be purchased fresh all year, Norwegians still preserve seasonal foods because they appreciate their taste.

Meat and game have always been important. A relatively extensive menu showcases dishes prepared with lamb (*får*), beef (*okse*), pork (*svin*), deer (*dyr*), reindeer (*reinsdyr*), and moose (*elg*), and to a lesser extent, turkey (*kalkun*), goose (*gås*), duck (*and*), goat (*geit*), hare (*sørhare*), and game birds. Norwegians are equally fond of meat that is fresh, salted, dried, or smoked, and eaten hot or cold. Much of the fresh meat is processed into sausage (*pølse*), ground meat (*kjøttdeig*), or the leaner version of ground meat (*karbonadedeig*), and cold cuts (*pålegg*). Assorted salted and dried meats (*spekemat*) are relished as daily fare or as party food.

Lamb is a favorite meat, and *får-i-kål* is the dish eagerly anticipated in autumn after the fattened sheep have been brought down from the mountains and butchered. *Får-i-kål* is a stew of fresh lamb, cabbage, and onions, laced with peppercorns. In the 1970s, this hearty stew was voted Norway's national dish. Befitting its importance, the dish was accorded a special day of recognition: the last Thursday in September, which is designated national *får-i-kål* day. Other prized lamb preparations include salted and dried leg of lamb (*fenalår*), which often is served in thin slices for the "cold table" (*koldtbord*), a buffet of cold dishes; and salted and dried lamb's ribs (*pinnekjøtt*), which are steamed over a rack of small birch sticks (*pinne*). Minced meat cakes (*kjøttkaker*) in the form of patties or balls are representative beef dishes. The meat is seasoned according to taste, often with ginger (*ingefær*) and nutmeg, and served in gravy. Another minced meat favorite, named "legless birds" (*benløse fugler*), is a dish of oblong stuffed meat rolls. The traditional stuffing is marrow and pork fat seasoned with ginger and cloves, but other stuffing choices include bacon or cured ham (*spekeskinke*), sometimes with chopped fruit. A thick beef stew (*bifflapskaus*) with root vegetables is a classic dish, as are the variations of it made with fresh lamb or salted meats. Pork is most often eaten as ham (*skinke*), bacon, sausage (*pølse*), or salt pork (*flesk*). Fried salt pork with apples (*epleflesk*) is a typical pork offering, as is fried salt pork served with boiled potatoes topped with a sauce made from the pork drippings (*flesk og duppe*). Roast pork with crisp rind (*svinestek med sprø svor*) is a delicious preparation made with fresh pork.

Wildlife is abundant in the mountains and forests, so it is not surprising that hunting is a popular sport in Norway. Reindeer (*reinsdyr*), red (*dyr*) and roe deer (*rådyr*), moose (*elg*), hare (*sørhare*), and grouse contribute to the supply of meat in the Norwegian diet. Fillet of reindeer (*reinsdyrfilet*) is popular, sometimes stuffed with brown cheese made from goat's milk whey (*geitost*). Stuffed boneless roast of roe deer (*farsert rådyrstek*), roast hare with lingonberries (*harestek med tyttebær*), and mountain ptarmigan (grouse) with juniper-flavored brown sauce (*rypa i gryta*) are just a few of the many game dish favorites.

The subject of eating whale (*hval*) must be broached because whale meat appears on menus and in butcher shops. Norway's whaling is limited to the Minke whale, which is not an endangered or threatened species—depending on whom you talk to. The Norwegian government registered an objection to the International Whaling Commission's commercial whaling moratorium, and consequently is not bound by it. The purpose of this guidebook is to inform, not to enter into the controversy of whaling. The reader must decide whether or not to eat the meat, which most often will be in the form of steaks (*hvalstek*). The same must be said for seal (*sel*), which typically is used in stews (*selgryte*).

Norway has never wanted for fish. Substantial quantities are caught in the sea along the extensive coastline, in the waters of the deep, long fjords, and in the plentiful lakes and rivers of the interior. Varieties such as cod (*torsk*), herring (*sild*), and salmon (*laks*) have long been an integral part of the cuisine. There also is a robust aquaculture industry. All of these riches are reflected in the large selection of fish and seafood dishes on the menu.

The importance of cod (*torsk*) as a mainstay of the Norwegian fishing industry cannot be overstated. For over a thousand years, fishermen on the northernmost coast of Norway have mined this gift from the sea. Although cod has been depleted by overfishing (not only in Norwegian waters) the overall catch is still substantial. At the end of January the arctic cod in the Barents Sea (called *skrei* in their spawning stage) migrate about 500 miles to their spawning grounds near the Lofoten and Vesterålen archipelagos above the Arctic Circle. Norwegians eagerly await the catch of scrumptious fresh cod at that time. The simple dish of poached cod with herbed butter (*kokt torsk med urtesmør*) is hard to resist, as is the more elegant "fish for a prince" (*prinsefisk*), a steamed cod fillet in white wine sauce served on a bed of asparagus spears. A whole boiled lobster (*hummer*) tail sits atop the fillet. Fried cod "tongues" (*sprøstekte torsketunger*) and cheeks (*friterte torskekinn*) are expensive delicacies. Many cod processing plants generously donate the

Norwegian arctic cod, one of Norway's most important foods throughout history. It was equally vital as a commodity for exportation.

heads to enterprising children, who cut off the cheeks and "tongues" and make good money selling them to connoisseurs.

A large portion of the cod caught off the Lofoten and Vesterålen islands is air-dried, using centuries-old techniques. Cod processing is the area's major industry. The cod migration occurs when the climate is ideal for air-drying the fish. Between February and May it is sunny, the temperature is above freezing, yet it is cold enough to prevent spoilage and insect infestation, and precipitation is low. Sizable catches during the spawning season make large-scale drying operations feasible. To produce dried fish (*stokkfisk*), the heads are removed first. Then the fish are gutted, tied together in pairs by the tail, and hung over poles, or sticks (*stokker*), to dry along the shore. Fish similarly prepared and hung on large wooden racks (*hjeller*) to dry are called *tørrfisk*, but the dried fish product is the same as *stokkfisk*. The shelf life of dried fish is several years. When a source of good-quality salt became available in the 17th century, the method of drying fish with salt began to be used as well. Salted, dried fish, especially cod, are called *klippfisk* ("cliff fish") because the fish were traditionally placed on rocky cliffs near the shore to dry in the summer sun and wind. Today commercial operations typically process the fish indoors in controlled-environment drying houses. Before the fish are dried, they are slit open along the spine up to the tail, and most of the backbone, the heads, and the entrails are removed. The flesh is spread open (butterflied) for optimal drying and then flattened into a more or less triangular shape.

Rehydrating dried cod is an easy but time-consuming process, entailing several days of soaking the fish in many changes of water. Once softened, the fish is very versatile. It appears in a variety of casseroles, including cod cooked with potatoes in a tomato-based sauce (*tørrfisk i tomatsaus*) and cod served in a creamy white sauce with mustard and capers (*tørrfisk med sennepssaus og kaperser*). The outstanding dish made with salt cod is *bacalao,* which is of Spanish origin. Sliced tomatoes, sweet bell peppers, and raw potatoes are alternately layered with pieces of fish, and simmered in water and olive oil.

Outside of Norway, lye-fish (*lutefisk*) is perhaps the most well-known Norwegian dish made with dried, unsalted cod. Although traditionally a Christmas dish, it may be enjoyed any time of the year. To prepare *lutefisk,* dried cod is softened in a solution of lye, followed by many rinses in water. The fish is poached in salted water and served topped with mustard sauce or with melted butter and bits of bacon. Boiled potatoes and crisp flatbread undoubtedly accompany it.

Norwegian salmon (*laks*) is recognized the world over for its high-quality, rich red flesh. Fresh, smoked, or cured, it is a highlight of the country's menu. Fresh poached salmon served with Sandefjord butter (*kokt laks med sandefjordsmør*) is outstanding. Sandefjord butter, a fish sauce made with cream, butter, lemon juice, and chives or parsley, was inspired by the composition of *beurre blanc*, a classic French sauce. The director of the Park Hotel in Sandefjord, Otto Fredik Borchgrevink, who had studied in Paris, reportedly created and named the sauce in the mid-1900s. Steamed salmon with cucumber salad and whipped sour cream (*dampet laks med agurksalat og pisket rømme*) and roasted salmon with honey and mustard (*ovnsstekt laks med honning og sennep*) are other popular ways to feature fresh salmon. Smoked salmon also is superb. Served with poached eggs, caviar, and capers on top of rye bread (*røykt laks med forlorent egg, rogn, og kaperser på rugbrød*), it is a very satisfying meal. A surprising number of foods are successfully paired with smoked salmon on open-face sandwiches. The same may be said for cured salmon (*gravlaks*), which is salmon that has been marinated for a few days in a mixture of salt, sugar, and dill, then served thinly sliced. The flavor of cured salmon is nicely enhanced by mustard sauce (*gravlaks med sennepssaus*).

Herring (*sild*) is another historically important everyday food, which is savored salted and dried (*spekesild*), pickled (*sursild*), and fresh (*fersk sild*). Popular preparations are salted herring with sour cream sauce (*spekesild med rømmesaus*), salted herring with onion and tomato (*spekesild med løk og tomat*), and old-fashioned pickled herring (*gammeldags sild*), which is brined in vinegar water with allspice berries, mustard seeds, peppercorns, and cloves. Crisp, fried fresh herring (*sprøstekt sild*) is a nice alternative to salted herring.

Other important fish in the traditional Norwegian diet include trout (*ørret*), mackerel (*makrell*), halibut (*kveite*), and sardines (*sardin*). Representative menu entries are fried whole trout (*stekt ørret*), mountain trout with herbed butter and warm potato and apple salad (*fjellørret med urtesmør og lun potet og eplesalat*), pickled mackerel (*syltet makrell*), and halibut cooked with cabbage (*kveite i kål*). Sardines usually are canned, but when eaten fresh they generally are smoked, grilled, or pickled. Canned sardines are made into a spread (*sardinpålegg*) for open-face sandwiches.

Freshwater fish, mostly trout and arctic char (*ishavsrøye*), are also fermented, using an age-old technique. Gutted fish, with gills removed but heads and tails intact, are submerged in weak brine for 2 to 3 months at low temperature. Flavor development depends on salt concentration, temperature, and the length of time the fish is fermented. Fish that are not brined with kidneys or blood present have a milder smell. Commercially prepared, vacuum-packed fermented fish (*rakfisk*) is available in mild, mature, or very mature varieties. *Rakfisk* are sliced and eaten raw, usually on flatbread, with sour cream sauce and boiled potatoes. Afficionados have their own social group: *Rakfiskens Venner* (Friends of *Rakfisk*).

Some species of fish only recently were deemed edible. Once tossed back into the water if caught, the unattractive monkfish or anglerfish (*breiflabb*) and the wolffish or arctic catfish (*steinbit*) now are highly regarded and appear on upscale restaurant menus. Their tasty flesh is savored in preparations such as herb-fried medallions of anglerfish (*urtestekt medaljonger av breiflabb*), fillet of arctic catfish with onions and capers (*steinbitfilet med løk og kaperser*), and oven-baked arctic catfish with mushroom sauce and carrot purée (*ovnsbakt steinbit med sjampinjongsaus og gulrotpuré*).

Norway never developed a tradition of eating raw fresh fish. And shellfish consumption has only become common in the 20th century. This was partly because fish were so abundant, and bringing in a catch of fish was less time-consuming than harvesting shellfish. Now Norwegians and tourists alike can be seen snacking on a heap of peel-your-own shrimp (*reker*) on top of a piece of bread, or in a bowl, with mayonnaise and lemon wedges on the side. Shrimp salad (*rekesalat*), shrimp balls (*rekeboller*), cauliflower with shrimp sauce (*blomkål med rekesaus*), and crab salad flavored with coriander (*krabbesalat med koriander*) are some of the possible seafood choices. Mussels are highlighted in creamy soups with white wine, lightly seasoned with saffron and curry (*blåskjellsuppe med safran og karri*).

Dairy products are a vital part of the Norwegian diet. Most Norwegians drink milk with every meal. Fine cheeses and dishes made from milk enrich the menu, and soured milk products, developed before refrigeration was available, remain extremely popular.

Sour cream (*rømme*) is a classic and popular food. It is the key ingredient in sour cream porridge (*rømmegrøt*), one of the oldest traditional dishes in Norway. *Tettemelk* is a thick, yogurt-like product originally made by pouring fresh milk over the leaves of the common butterwort plant. Lactic acid bacteria on the leaves cause the milk to acidify and curdle. Soured whey (*syra*), an old-time beverage still drunk today, is made from the liquid that separates from the curds during cheese production. *Blanda,* another beverage with deep historical roots, is also made from soured whey (or soured milk) mixed with water. A unique and very old dish, *gomme* is a sweet milk dessert that is very time-consuming to prepare. The milk must simmer without stirring for about five hours. At this stage, thick and a light golden color, the milk is slowly added to beaten eggs and brown sugar. Rural homes or fairs may still offer an opportunity to sample *gomme*.

Butter (*smør*) had been so valuable a commodity in Norway that it once was negotiable currency. Elaborate butter sculptures were displayed at important gatherings where food was served. The hand-carved wooden molds used to make butter sculptures are coveted collector's items today.

Gammelost ("old cheese") is a cow's milk cheese with a long history in Norway. It is a pungent, brownish-yellow, granular cheese made from skim milk that is soured prior to being heated. Soured milk curdles naturally without rennet, and the curds produced are pressed into forms. When the cheese is removed from the forms, it is inoculated with a mold, typically *Penicillium roqueforti,* which produces greenish-blue veining and the characteristic strong flavor and aroma of the cheese. It keeps for long periods without refrigeration. *Gammelost* was made commercially for over a century in a single dairy in the western municipality of Vik in the county of Sogn og Fjordane, but production has now expanded to other counties.

The Norwegians were particularly inventive when it came to making cheeses from whey. *Brunost* is the general term for brown whey cheese. To make the cheese, the whey, sometimes with a little whole milk or cream added, is boiled for 8–10 hours. As the water boils off, the whey proteins react with lactose sugar to produce a delicious cheese that is brown, slightly caramelized, and somewhat sweet. After the cheese mass cools it is pressed into square wooden molds, whose inner surfaces have carved designs that become imprinted on the cheese block. Traditionally, *brunost* is made with goat's-milk whey and is called *geitost*. Strictly speaking, if the whey contains no additives, the cheese is called *mysost* or *ekte* (pure) *geitost*. If the cheese is made from cow's-milk whey it is called *fløtemysost*. A block of brown whey cheese will certainly be on the table for most meals in Norway, accompanied by a cheese plane (a Norwegian invention) for shaving neat, wafer-thin slices for open-face sandwiches. *Eggost* (egg cheese) is a cheese dessert. A well-beaten mixture of eggs, soured milk, and sugar is added to boiling milk. The curds that form are strained and served topped with a drizzle of cinnamon and sugar.

Norway is self-sufficient in root vegetables, which have a long history in Norwegian cookery. The carrot (*gulrot*), turnip (*nepe*), parsnip (*pastinakk*),

Old wooden mold used to press goat's-milk cheeses. From the collection of Undredal Stølsysteri, a small cooperative dairy in the village of Undredal along the Aurlandsfjord in western Norway.

cabbage (*kål*), rutabaga, also known as Swede (*kålrabi; kålrot*), onion (*løk*), celeriac (*sellerirot*), kohlrabi (*knutekål*), Jerusalem artichoke (*jordskokk*), and black salsify root (*skorsonerrot*) store well and are ingrained in the diet. The rutabaga is called the "Nordic orange" because it is high in vitamin C. Notably, *kålrabi* is not the name for kohlrabi; it is one of the names for rutabaga.

The potato was introduced to Norway in the 1750s and became a daily staple in the early 1800s. Its assimilation was hastened by the failure of grain harvests. As ubiquitous as the potato is at mealtimes, it is a little amazing that one recipe served for so long. Potatoes traditionally are boiled whole, unpeeled, and are served with or without their skins, with a garnish of chopped fresh parsley, usually without butter. Perhaps varying the type of potato that was cooked was enough variety for most people. Chopped potatoes are in many traditional soups and stews, but global influences have put mashed, scalloped, fried, and baked preparations on many of today's menus. Potatoes are an essential ingredient in some types of soft flatbread (*lefse*) and are the basis for the beloved grated-potato dumpling (*komle*), which usually is eaten on Thursdays for reasons that remain a mystery.

Vegetables (*grønnsaker*) have become considerably more important in the Norwegian diet over the last fifty years. They are no longer simply side dishes, and salads (*salat*) are common. Favorite salad makings include lettuce (*salat*), tomato (*tomat*), cucumber (*agurk*), onion (*løk*), and radish (*reddik*). Carrots (*gulrøtter*) are also popular as snacks, eaten raw or pickled. An interesting combination is carrots pickled in orange juice (*appelsinsyltet gulrot*). A greater variety of produce has been made available by the canning and freezing industries, and today just about anything can be imported fresh.

Most vegetables served hot have been boiled. A side dish of carrots is fairly common, as is their addition to stews and soups to provide flavor and color. Rutabaga (*kålrot*) is most often served mashed (*kålrotstappe*). Norway's pickled version of sauerkraut (*surkål*), cabbage cooked with vinegar, sugar, and caraway (*karve*), is a runaway favorite. Cabbage (*kål*) also reigns with lamb (*får*) in the national autumn dish *får-i-kål*. The Jerusalem artichoke (*jordskokk*), once a staple, has largely been supplanted by the potato. But it can be sampled in a dish of creamed Jerusalem artichokes topped with a poached egg (*stuete jordskokker med forlorent egg*). Broccoli (*brokkoli*), cauliflower (*blomkål*), and Brussels sprouts (*rosenkål*) are also newer additions to Norwegian cookery.

Only recently have mushrooms (*sopp*) been considered important enough to use in cooking. Although gathering wild mushrooms is a popular activity, cultivated mushrooms are far more commonly used in cooking. Representative dishes are mushroom soup (*soppsuppe*) and fillet of reindeer on a bed of creamed leeks and mushrooms (*reinsdyrfilet på puree og soppseng*).

Fruits are cultivated in private and commercial orchards. They are made into jams, jellies, marmalades, snacks, and desserts. Apples (*epler*) are by far the major fruit crop, and since the growing season is cool and short, only early-maturing varieties can be grown successfully. "Veiled peasant girls" (*tilslørte bondepiker*), a layered dish of caramelized bread crumbs, stewed apples, and whipped cream, is a dessert loved throughout Norway. The name of this dessert suggests that a fancy dish has been concocted from ordinary ingredients. The top layer of cream is the "veil." Another national favorite is fruit soup (*fruktsuppe*) made with whatever fresh, frozen, and dried fruits are at hand. *Fruktsuppe* is served warm or cold. Other orchard-grown fruits are pears (*pærer*), plums (*plommer*), cherries (*kirsebær*), apricots (*aprikoser*), and peaches (*ferskener*).

Each year young and old alike look forward to the berry-picking season. Norwegian berries have particularly robust flavors, which are attributed to slow maturation in the cold climate. Strawberries (*jordbær*) are a welcome harbinger of summer and are always delicious plain, sugared, or with sweetened cream. Strawberries growing in the north begin to ripen just as the season is over in the south. Raspberries (*bringebær*), red currants (*rips*), and black currants (*solbær*) also are garden-grown.

Wild berries are found in woodlands all over Norway, and berry-gathering is a national pastime in the summer and autumn. The amber-colored cloudberry (*multebær*), not always easy to find, is especially sought after. Each raspberry-like berry grows at the end of a branchless stalk, and when a cloudberry patch is discovered, the location is unlikely to be divulged. The dessert of cloudberries mixed with whipped cream and sugar (*multekrem*) is a tasty reward for a successful hunt. Should cloudberries remain elusive, there are blueberries (*blåbær*), lingonberries (*tyttebær*), mountain crowberries (*fjellkrekling*), blackberries (*bjørnebær*), rowanberries (*rognebær*), and juniper berries (*einebær*) to pick. Woodland strawberries (*markjordbær*) and raspberries (*markbringebær*) are tiny, intensely flavored versions of their cultivated counterparts. Berries are eaten fresh, made into jams, jellies, juices, toppings, sauces, cakes, and other desserts, added to pancake and waffle batters, or frozen for later use. Sauces made with wild berries are considered excellent complements to game dishes.

Norway imports a large assortment of fresh fruit that cannot be grown in its cold climate. Melons, grapes, tropical, citrus, and dried fruits such as raisins, dates, and figs are widely available.

Few flavor enhancements are added to traditional Norwegian dishes. The natural tastes of food are much preferred over aromatic spices and seasonings. An exception is caraway (*karve*). Caraway flavors Norway's version of sauerkraut (*surkål*); a traditional sour milk cheese (*pultost*) made with cow's milk; and is also the basis of a soup (*karvekålsuppe*) that contains either finely chopped young taproots and leaves of the caraway plant, or sprouted caraway seeds. Caraway is used in baked goods such as *surbrød,* a round, flat, sour bread, and to flavor the distilled alcoholic beverage aquavit (*akevitt*). Dill is the seasoning of choice for curing fish, especially salmon (*laks*). The popular fish pudding *fiskepudding* is seasoned with dill. Marinades and pickling solutions have dill, and cooked, fresh spring vegetables often are garnished with sprigs of dill. Juniper berries flavor some meats and vegetables, and sauces containing them traditionally pair with game. If used whole, juniper berries are usually removed after cooking. Parsley (*persille*), most visible as a chopped garnish on top of boiled potatoes, is found in a wide range of dishes, including the recent "classic," Sandefjord butter (*Sandefjordsmør*). Black peppercorns (*svarte pepperkorn*) are enjoyed for the rich flavor they impart as they soften during cooking. The national favorite dish, *får-i-kål*, is lamb and cabbage stew flavored with black peppercorns. Mustard (*sennep*) is the primary flavor in the sauce that usually accompanies cured salmon (*gravlaks*). Ginger (*ingefær*), nutmeg (*muskat*), cloves (*nellik*), cardamom (*kardemomme*), cinnamon (*kanel*), and saffron (*safran*) have long been used in Norwegian cooking, originally among the elite, and their usage was not limited to sweet baked goods. Stuffed pork loin with prune sauce (*fylt svinekam med sviskesaus*) and fried pork patties (*medisterkaker*) are flavored with ginger. Both ginger and cloves are in the traditional stuffing of meat rolls (*benløse fugler*). Meat patties with creamed cabbage (*kjøttkaker med stuet kål*) contain a mixture of ginger and nutmeg. The flavor of nutmeg is also imparted to fish preparations, including fish au gratin (*fiskegrateng*). Cardamom appears in savory foods such as the flour and egg dumplings (*melboller*) that are added to clear soups, and saffron is paired with cinnamon to flavor roasted chicken (*høne*).

Traditional Norwegian bread is unleavened, crisp flatbread made from barley, oats, or rye. Dough containing flour, salt, and water is rolled out into wafer-thin, roughly circular pieces, which are then cooked on a griddle. Dry flatbread keeps for a long time if stored properly. Historically, it was the solution to the problem of moldy flour. On farms in the past, flatbread and other preserved foods were kept in a special storehouse (*stabbur*) to stay dry over the winter. The *stabbur* was raised on stilts to minimize rodent infestation. Around 1900, oven-baked, leavened bread became the standard. Flatbread remains popular, however, and is available commercially. The flatbread baking tradition is kept alive in some rural parts of the country, often as a communal effort in the fall after the grain is harvested.

Soft, griddle-fried flatbread (*lefse*) also has deep historical roots. It was served on special occasions and still is popular today. Regional variations in composition and configuration abound. *Lefse* may be made from one kind of flour or a mixture of flours. Mashed potatoes are added to the dough in certain regions. Some *lefse* recipes include eggs, milk, syrup, or yeast. A grooved rolling pin is used to shape the dough, which helps minimize bubbling in the *lefse* while frying. *Lefse* most often is buttered and sprinkled with sugar, but many other spreads are used. Before it is eaten, *lefse* is rolled up, folded over and cut into pieces, or arranged in multilayered constructions.

Pillared wooden storehouse (*stabbur*) dating to the 1600s. It is one of several old buildings on Sevletunet, a farm in western Norway, which is now protected by the Norwegian Heritage Foundation.

Some types of *lefse* are dried and stored for later use. Dried *lefse* is softened for meals by running water over it and allowing it to rest on a moist towel for about 15 minutes. A soft, potato-based *lefse* (*lompe*) serves as a hot dog wrapper in the fast-food market.

Bread (*brød*) is an integral part of most daily meals. A large selection of leavened breads and rolls are available. Popular loaves are *grovbrød,* a coarse dark rye bread; *kneippbrød,* whole-wheat bread; *grahambrød,* graham-flour bread; and the trendy *speltbrød* made with spelt, an ancient, high-protein grain. White bread (*loff*) is also common. Much of the bread is used to make open-face sandwiches (*smørbrød*), for which there are an infinite variety of toppings (*pålegg*), including jams and jellies, pickled herring, smoked fish, hard-boiled eggs, an assortment of cured meats, and cheeses, especially brown goat's milk cheese. A relatively recent tradition is the packed lunch (*matpakke*) of open-face sandwiches that accompanies school children and business people alike.

Grains are also used to make porridges (*grøter*), such as sour-cream porridge (*rømmegrøt*). Flour is added to the sour cream (*rømme*) to thicken it, and the porridge is cooked until the butterfat separates out and floats on top. In the summer it is often eaten with cured meat and flatbread. Indicative of its high regard, *rømmegrøt* was given as a present to celebrate important occasions such as births and weddings, delivered in special lidded wooden baskets that were often elaborately decorated with rosemaling. In the past, everyday porridge (*grøt*) choices were barley (*bygg*) and oats (*havre*), which were cooked with water and sometimes eaten with soured milk. Porridges based on rice (*ris*) or semolina (*semulegryn*) were eaten on special occasions. Once standard daily fare in Norway for centuries, porridges have largely given way to packaged breakfast cereals. *Rømmegrøt* remains important for special occasions.

Although potato consumption remains high, global trends have pushed pasta and rice onto the everyday menu. And frozen pizza has become enormously popular, especially among younger Norwegians.

Sweets are enjoyed for dessert or between meals with coffee (*kaffe*). Fruit (*frukt*) is often featured. Sweet fruit soup (*fruktsuppe*) and a milk-based dessert such as velvety caramel pudding (*karamellpudding*) are always popular. Berries and berry sauces are perennial favorites, especially the dessert of cloudberries and whipped cream (*multekrem*). Another berry dessert, *trollkrem,* is a mixture of beaten egg whites and sugar, usually mixed with lingonberries. Waffles with jam (*vafler med syltetøy*) are served as a dessert, and they most often are made in a waffle iron that makes five connected heart-shaped waffles.

Cakes (*kaker*) are typically served at coffee time and take center stage on festive occasions and holidays. Among the many delicious choices is a layered sponge cake (*bløtkake*) filled with whipped cream and fruit, and iced with whipped cream. "Royalty cake" (*fyrstekake*) has a pastry layer covered with rich, chewy, cardamom-flavored almond paste and is topped with a lattice of pastry strips. Almond wreath cake (*kransekake*) is a spectacular ring cake made of ground almonds, sugar, and egg whites, typically made for the Christmas holidays. Successively smaller rings of baked dough are stacked on top of each other and held together with icing, producing a cone-shaped cake. Another perennial holiday classic is the traditional sheet cake sprinkled with sugar, dried currants, and almonds known as *Mor Monsen* (Mother Monsen), whose identity has been lost to history.

Cookies (*småkaker*) are served at coffee time throughout the year, but during the Christmas season expect special cookies. A few of the author's traditional favorites are shortbread-like cookies shaped like a wreath (*Berlinerkranser*) and the crispy, deep-fried rosettes (*rosettbakkelser*) made with a special rosette iron (*rosettbakkelsjern*). *Rosettbakkelser* are sprinkled with powdered sugar or topped with whipped cream and jam. Also high on her list are deep-fried "poor man's cookies" (*fattigmann bakkelser*) sprinkled with powdered sugar. To form their characteristic knotted appearance, diamond-shaped pieces of rolled dough are slit lengthwise in the center, and one point of the diamond is pulled through the slit. Crispy, flat, waffle cookies (*krumkaker*) are likely to be on everyone's favorite traditional Christmas cookie list. They are cooked in a special two-sided iron, which forms a design on each side. When golden brown, the cookies are removed from the iron and quickly rolled into tubes or cones. *Krumkaker* are eaten plain or filled, typically with whipped cream.

The beverage of choice is milk (*melk*), with coffee (*kaffe*) running a close second. Most people have a glass of milk with meals, and children drink it after school, choosing either whole milk (*helmelk* or *h-melk*), low-fat milk (*lettmelk*), skim milk (*skummetmelk*), or cultured milk (*kulturmelk*). Norwegians love their bottomless cup of strong coffee (mainly black), which they drink after meals, with desserts, and with alcoholic beverages. People routinely invite friends to their home to enjoy coffee and cake together, or savor coffee and dessert with them at a dinner party. Not surprisingly, coffee shops are everywhere. Tea (*te*) is less popular than coffee. Many different types of fruit and berries are used to make juice. In its concentrated form, juice is called *saft*. Consumption of carbonated soft drinks (*leskedrikker*) has risen dramatically in the years since Norway has become an affluent country.

Norway's national drink is aquavit, a high-proof (42–45 percent alcohol by volume), caraway-flavored beverage now distilled from potatoes. Until the potato got a foothold in the country, aquavit was a grain-based spirit. Its name is derived from the Latin *aqua vitae,* meaning "the water of life." The most popular alcoholic drink consumed with food, aquavit is served chilled in small glasses, often chased with beer. Those who are unlikely to imbibe aquavit during the year probably will have a customary drink at Christmas. Three categories of aquavit are produced: classic, regional, and special, and their variety and specificity are considerable. Some aquavits are meant to be paired with certain foods. The specific pairing is indicated in the name on the label. For example, Opland Rakefisk is to be drunk with fermented fish. The most widely known brand of aquavit outside Norway is Linie Aquavit. This spirit is aged in the holds of ships in oak barrels used previously for sherry and is shipped to Australia and back before it is sold, thus crossing the equator ("line") twice. As the story goes, this method of aging was empirically determined. Unsold aquavit brought back from Australia was found to have improved flavor. This was attributed to the cumulative effect on the casks of the gentle rocking of the ship, temperature fluctuations en route, and the longer duration of a round trip. Even today, casks of Linie Aquavit make this same long voyage. The label on each bottle of Linie Aquavit gives an accounting of its travels, including the name of the transporting ship.

Beer (*øl*) has played a prominent role in Norwegian society since before the Christian era. Interesting accounts and laws relating to brewing beer and its consumption are contained in many of the sagas of the Norwegian kings as early as the 12th century. By the 19th century, commercial breweries were producing beer that traditionally had been made in individual households. The most popular variety of beer in Norway is pilsner, a type of light lager brewed and stored at low temperatures. Munkholm is a popular brand of alcohol-free beer. *Juleøl* is a malty, dark beer brewed only at Christmastime.

Of course, wine (*vin*) is very popular, too, but Norway's climate is not conducive to growing grapes. A wide selection of fine imported wines is available. Since 1922 the Norwegian government has controlled the sales of alcoholic beverages through its *Vinmonopolet* (Wine Monopoly). It is the only retail outlet in the country for alcoholic bottled and canned goods with greater than 4.75 percent alcohol by volume. *Vinmonopolet* stores can be found throughout the country, but their hours of operation are somewhat limited. Low-alcohol beer may be sold in grocery stores.

The Regions of Norway

Norway was redistricted in the early 1900s, replacing the traditional districts based on geographical elements such as fjords, valleys, and mountain ranges with a modern system of formal administrative units. Many of the traditional districts only partially coincided with the new geographical boundaries. Under the modern system, Norway and the thousands of offshore islands along her western flank were divided into 5 major regions. These regions were further subdivided into a total of 19 counties, which themselves were divided into a total of 430 municipalities. It helps to understand both the traditional districting system of Norway and the modern system of formal administrative units, because the names of many traditional dishes include old regional references.

Western Norway (Vestlandet)

Western Norway is parceled into four counties: Møre og Romsdal, Sogn og Fjordane, Hordaland, and Rogaland. This narrow coastal region is mountainous and renowned for its spectacular fjords and the many dramatic waterfalls that plummet down their steep-walled cliffs into the sea. Numerous small, rocky outcroppings called skerries shelter the coast. The climate is milder than would be expected at this latitude because of the warming effect of the Gulf Stream. Much rain falls in the Norwegian fjords and snowfall is rare, even in winter. Located at the southern tip of Vestlandet is the lowland Jæren plain, which is one of Norway's major agricultural areas. Field crops such as vegetables, potatoes, and cereals are grown here, and extensive greenhouse farming produces warmer-weather crops such as tomatoes and bell peppers. A small, local variety of garden pea, which used to be sown with oats to enrich the nitrogen content of the soil, is now at risk of extinction. To call attention to this heirloom variety, the Slow Food organization has included the Jæren pea in its Ark of Taste. Slow Food is also watching *Vossakvann,* the archangel Gabriel's herb, a cultivated variety of wild mountain angelica (*Angelica archangelica*) with solid stalks. This herb, which has been used since at least the 11th century, today is found only in the municipality of Voss in Hordaland county. *Vossakvann* is used in salads or made into a pesto sauce (*englarøra*) by blanching some sprigs and then puréeing them with olive oil in a blender.

The mountain slopes along the fjords are well-suited to horticulture. Hardanger, the traditional district surrounding Hardangerfjord, is Norway's orchard, producing about 40 percent of the nation's fruit. Domestically grown apples, pears, plums, cherries, apricots, and peaches found in the country's markets are likely to have come from this district. Juice from Hardanger apples has Protected Designation of Origin (PDO) status; only juice made from these apples may carry the Hardanger name, and the entire production process must occur in Hardanger. A sparkling apple cider (*Hardanger Sider Sprudlande*) made in the town of Ulvik is sold in the *Vinmonopolet*. *Pærer fra Hardanger* is a Hardanager dessert of pear halves stewed in water with lingonberry jam, sugar, and cinnamon, served with crispy waffle cookies and whipped cream.

Wildlife is plentiful in western Norway. Deer, red deer, and moose are found in forested areas, and herds of reindeer are common on the Hardanger Plateau (*Hardangervidda*), a barren expanse above the tree line. A regional hunter's stew (*jegergryte*) contains venison or reindeer, bacon, and prunes. Game birds are avidly hunted. Mountain ptarmigan is featured in a specialty of the municipality of Voss, *ripa i gryta,* in which the fowl is cooked with milk and brown goat cheese and served with juniper-flavored brown sauce.

The mountainous terrain of western Norway is more suited to raising sheep and goats than cattle. Among the regional meat dishes is a traditional fall and Christmas preparation of lamb called *smalahove,* which is highly regarded by local Norwegians, but not by many tourists. A lamb's head (with brains removed) is salted, smoked, and boiled. Half a head is plated with mashed rutabagas and a whole, unpeeled, boiled potato. Another specialty of the region showcasing salted and dried lamb is *pinnekjøtt,* lamb's ribs steamed in a pot over small birch sticks (*pinne*). It also is a typical Christmas dish. Sausage is a popular product from the municipality of Voss. Its signature smoked links (*Vossakorv*) containing a mixture of beef, pork, and lamb have wide appeal and are an integral part of many dishes.

Villages along the Sognefjord and Aurlandsfjord, a branch of the Sognefjord, continue a 500-year tradition of producing cheese from raw goat's milk. The main area of cheese production is Undredal. Artisanal brown cheeses are made from goat's milk whey. The *geitost* production in these villages is under the protection of a Slow Food Presidium, which promotes and provides support for traditional, small-scale production of quality foods.

Several important coastal cities in western Norway came into existence because of the abundance of fish in the sea. Kristiansund's history is closely tied to the cod industry, and in particular dried salt cod (*klippfisk*). In the 18th century, Spanish merchants trading in *klippfisk* introduced their salt cod preparation, *bacalao*. The dish, which contains potatoes and tomatoes, became one of Kristiansund's classic specialties. Ålesund, Norway's principal fishing port, was at the center of the herring (*sild*) industry. Stavanger, now the hub of Norway's oil industry, once had a vibrant fish canning factory, which is well documented in the city's Canning Museum. Herring, brisling, and sardine packing provided employment for more than half the city. A preparation of salted herring topped with an egg, mustard sauce, and vinegar sauce (*Stavangersild*) is one of Stavanger's local offerings.

The second largest city in Norway, Bergen, has a long history of trade in dried cod, and had been one of the Hanseatic League's main trading posts. Among the several dishes attributed to Bergen is a fish soup (*Bergensk fiskesuppe*) made with a type of cod called saithe (*sei*), carrots, and celery root in a sweet-and-sour broth thickened with cream and egg yolk.

Soft flatbread (*lefse*) variations in western Norway include *krotakake,* an attractive, patterned version made from a yeast dough of wheat or rye flour and sometimes mashed potatoes. A conventional rolling pin is used to make thin circles of dough, which are scored in perpendicular directions with a special grooved rolling pin (*krotakakekjevle*). This forms a characteristic grid in the dough and prevents the formation of air pockets during frying. *Krotakake* typically is spread with a mixture of butter and sugar, and sometimes whipped cream, then rolled up. This version of *lefse,* also called

Grooved, metal rolling pin (*krotakakekjevle*) used to create the grid pattern on *krotakake,* a type of soft flatbread (*lefse*) made in western Norway. From the collection of Jon Grinde, Madison, Wisconsin, whose great-grandmother Jorand Asbjornsdatter Instenes, from the municipality of Loftus, was the pin's original owner. Photographed with permission.

Hardangerbrød, comes from Hardanger. *Sveler,* leavened griddle-fried pancakes made with cultured milk, are a specialty of the traditional district of Sunnmøre in Møre og Romsdal county in western Norway. They are spread with butter and sugar, jam, or cheese, and folded in half. *Sveler* are a popular fast food on the ferries in the Sunnmøre fjords. Bergen's fame in the dessert category rests especially on a multilayered sponge cake (*hvit dame*) that has a luscious filling of strawberry jam and whipped cream between each layer. Elegant touches include a layer of macaroon with hazelnuts placed near the bottom of the cake and a layer of marzipan that completely covers the whipped-cream icing.

Southern Norway (Sølandet or Agder)

The region of southern Norway has two counties, Vest-Agder and Aust-Agder, which lie on the southern tip of Norway. The region includes many islands and skerries along the coast. It is a relatively small region with only about 5.5 percent of the country's population, and almost 80 percent of the region's inhabitants live along the coast. Valleys and rivers are oriented in a north-south direction. Southern Norway is the nation's sunbelt and, not surprisingly, the climate is milder than elsewhere in the country. Snow does fall in the region, but it does not last long on the coast.

Agriculture and forestry are the major sources of income in the region. Sizable forests not too far from the sea support a thriving lumber industry. Commercial fishing is also strong. The region is known for its mackerel, but salmon, shrimp, crab, and herring are also important. Storelva River, which runs from Lake Vegår in Aust-Agder to the sea near Tvedestrand, is the place to be for anglers looking to catch sea trout (*sjøørret*) and salmon. Norway's southernmost town, Mandal, is in Vest-Agder in the municipality of the same name. The town's development was closely tied with the salmon industry as can be seen in its coat-of-arms, which prominently depicts three salmon. Cattle and sheep are pastured inland, and moose are abundant in the municipality of Songdalen in Vest-Anger. Farmers in the area can get a head start on planting their crops because of the more favorable climate. Important crops on the small farms include barley, potato, turnip, asparagus, and melon.

Typical fish preparations of southern Norway are mackerel soup (*makrellsuppe*) and pickled mackerel (*syltet makrell fra Sørlandet*). Another is fish balls (*fiskemat på Sørlandsvis*). Beef and pork are featured in a cabbage soup attributed to Aust-Agder (*kålsuppe fra Aust-Agder*), which also contains kohlrabi and barley. Another classic dish, *nepespa,* contains rutabagas and cured lamb. After the lamb and rutabagas have been boiled, they are set aside and the broth is thickened with flour and milk. The meat, rutabagas, and thickened broth are served separately. *Nepespa* is a traditional Christmas dish from Valle, a municipality in Aust-Agder, and it is served with the local soft flatbread (*lefse*) made with potatoes. A regional potato *lefse* (*klinelefse fra Aust-Agder)* is fried and spread with an egg-and-milk mixture or with unpasteurized milk. The *lefse* is refried to dry the spread. A specialty sausage (*mårpølse*) is made from moose meat and heart. Carrot soup comes from Flekkerøy (*gulrotsuppe fra Flekkerøy*), a small island in Vest-Agder, close to Kristiansand and connected to it by a tunnel. Sister cake (*søsterkake*), a buttery yeast cake with raisins and ground cardamom, is a sweet from Vest-Agder. Fevik rhubarb (*Fevikrabarbra*) is a dish of sweetened rhubarb and cream from the village of Fevik in the municipality of Grimstad in Aust-Agder.

Eastern Norway (Østlandet)

There are eight counties in eastern Norway: Telemark, Buskerud, Hedmark, Oppland, Akershus, Oslo, Vestfold, and Østfold. The eastern region of Norway is mountainous and heavily forested. The main mountain range is the Jotunheimen, which lies across the center of the country, straddling the boundary between Sogn of Fjordane county in western Norway and Oppland county in eastern Norway. Twenty seven of the highest peaks in Norway are in the Jotunheimen, including Galdhøpiggen, the crown of the range at 8,100 feet. Valleys run east to west, and most are cut into mountains. A substantial lowland area of lakes and fertile valleys surrounds Oslo, which is both a county and the nation's capital. The area around Oslofjord, with metropolitan Oslo at its apex, has the highest population density in the country. Over 40 percent of the people reside here. Eastern Norway has a continental climate with cold winters, warm summers, and moderate rainfall.

Agriculture is central to eastern Norway's economy. Rich soils and a favorable climate have made prosperous farming possible in many areas throughout the region, especially in the area east of Lake Mjøsa, Norway's largest lake, which lies between the counties of Hedmark and Oppland. Farms in Hedmark county are often huge, a remnant of the days when tenant farmers worked the fields of a wealthy landowner. More grain (wheat, barley, and oats) and potatoes are grown in Hedmark than anywhere else in Norway. Almond potatoes (*mandelpotet*) are the most commonly grown variety. These oval, mild-tasting potatoes are considered a delicacy. Vegetables, fruits, and berries are also cultivated. The municipality of Ringerike in Buskerud county is known for two vegetables: the Ringerike potato (*Ringerikspotet*) and the Ringerike pea (*Ringeriksert*). The potato is small with red skin and yellow flesh, and its flavor is considered superb. The pea is an old heritage vegetable that the Norwegian Seed Savers organization has successfully conserved through active cultivation by amateur gardeners. Both products are commercially available and have received PDO status.

Livestock farming includes cattle, goats, sheep, pigs, and poultry. Many herds of cattle and sheep are taken to summer dairy farms (*setrer*) in the mountains to utilize the pastures there, following centuries-old practices originally intended to preserve pastureland near the farms for growing winter fodder. A traditional dairy product still made at *setrer* is *pultost,* a soft, low-fat, sour-milk cheese made from cow's milk that is curdled with lactic acid bacteria rather than with rennet. It is lightly salted and flavored with caraway seeds. The cheese has a strong taste that sharpens with aging. Originally produced in many regions in Norway, *pultost* today is essentially a product associated with Oppland and Hedmark counties. It is another Norwegian artisanal cheese given Slow Food Presidium status to safeguard its continual production. The well-known Jarlsberg cheese is a Norwegian product. This mild "baby Swiss" cheese made with cow's milk was produced using expertise brought to Norway in 1830 by Swiss master cheesemakers. Production ceased after a few years, but resumed in 1956. The cheese was named Jarlsberg in 1961 after Jarlsberg and Laurvig county (now Vestfold county) in eastern Norway, where the cheese was originally made. A much-appreciated, salty butter, *Kviteseidsmør,* was originally produced in the municipality of Kviteseid in Telemark county. Although production has moved to a small village in the municipality of Bygland in Aust-Auger, southern Norway, *Kviteseidsmør* is still made the old-fashioned way.

Wildlife is plentiful in eastern Norway. Moose, roe deer, red deer, reindeer, and black grouse are among the hunted quarry.

Lake Mjøsa is home to many species of fish, including pike (*gjedde*), European perch (*abbor*), European whitefish or vendace (*lagesild*), and bream (*brasme*). Trout fermented in brine (*rakfisk*) is a specialty of the traditional district of Valdres in Oppland county. A consortium of six manufacturers produces it using traditional methods. The product (*rakfisk fra Valdres*) has PDO status.

A typical dish from eastern Norway is *småmat*. This clear soup with finely diced meat, vegetables, and potatoes comes from Hallingdal, a traditional district in Buskerud county. Telemark country offers *stekt flesk og duppe,* a dish of fried slices of salt pork with boiled potatoes. A sauce (*duppe*), made by whisking milk into the hot pork drippings, is ladled over the potatoes. From Tynset, a municipality in Hedmark county that is within the traditional region of Østerdalen, comes the dish of minced meat and onions cooked in water (*Østerdalshakk*). The meat and onions are taken out of the cooking liquid and are served with potatoes and vegetables. In Østvold, almond potatoes are mashed and served with a lamb shank cooked with carrots and celeriac (*lammeskank med mandelpotetmos fra Østvold*). Fried mushrooms are served on the side. Moose patties (*elgkarbonader fra Hedmark*) are a favorite in Hedmark. A dish of stewed salt pork and potatoes (*silpo*) is representative of the Solør area in Hedmark, home to people of Finnish extraction whose ancestors emigrated there in the 17th century. Among the fish entrées are herring soup (*sildesuppe*) from Oppland county and a layered fish pudding (*marmorert fiskepudding*) thickened with potato starch from Akershus county. To construct the pudding, half the mixture is tinted pink and alternating layers of tinted and untinted pudding are placed in a pan and baked.

Dessert selections include a "tower tart" (*tårn-tærte*) built from a stack of almond wafer cookies of increasingly smaller diameter held together with a layer of thick jam and glazed with powdered sugar. This treat comes from Akershus county. Also delicious is Vestfold county's bishop cake (*biskopkake*) made of whipped eggs and sugar, flour, almonds, and raisins. A type of flat, crispy cookie (*avlett*) made of barley flour is fried in a special pastry iron to create a delicate pattern on each side. *Avlett* is regional specialty of Gudbrandsdalen in Oppland county. Although the cuisine of Oslo leans toward international fare, there are some local offerings such as Sunday cake (*Søndagskake fra Oslo*), a buttery coconut cake with a glaze of powdered sugar and cocoa.

Jarlsberg, a popular, mild "baby Swiss" cow's-milk cheese. It has a distinctive nutty taste and characteristic large holes.

Central Norway (Trøndelag or Midt-Norge)

Two counties comprise central Norway: Sør-Trøndelag and Nord-Trøndelag. At the center of Sør-Trøndelag county is Norway's third largest fjord, the long, wide Trondheimsfjord, which extends a little over 80 miles inland. Several rivers drain into the fjord, including the Gaula and Orklæva, which are among the best salmon rivers in Norway. Abundant wetlands along the eastern boundary of the fjord provide habitat for game birds. The lowland valleys east and south of the fjord are productive agricultural areas with farms scattered throughout. The dominant crops are barley, oats, and potatoes. Cattle, sheep, and goats are raised for meat and milk. Raising sheep is a large-scale operation in the municipality of Oppdal in the south, which has the southeastern part of the Trollheimen mountain range within its boundaries. There are more sheep in Oppdal than any other municipality in the county. In the forests there are moose, reindeer, and roe deer. The westernmost municipality, Frøya, contains Frøya island and several thousand small islands surrounding it. Frøya island as well as nearby Hitra island, also a municipality, are key players in Norway's aquaculture industry, especially salmon farming. Hitra is home to a large population of deer. The climate of Sør-Trøndelag is highly variable. On the coast the summers are cool and the winters mild, but inland the climate is continental with temperature extremes and little precipitation.

Røros is an historic copper-mining town within the municipality of Røros, which lies at the eastern end of the county and shares a border with Sweden. In 1984, UNESCO included Røros in its World Heritage list. The historic smelting district as well as about 80 homes and other buildings in the town's central district have been preserved.

The municipality of Røros is famous for its organic sour cream (rømme), which is rich (high-fat), thick, and not homogenized. A thick, yogurt-like product (tettemelk) was originally made by pouring fresh milk over the leaves of the common butterwort plant. Lactic acid bacteria on the leaves increase the milk's acidity, causing it to curdle. Rørosfe, or black-sided Trønder og Nordland, once the dominant breed of cows in the area, are being raised today to produce organic milk. The breed typically has black and white spots, and a large patch of black on at least one of its sides. These small cows produce less milk, but can graze on scrub grass.

Most of Nord-Trøndelag is lower than 2,000 feet above sea level. Forty percent of the county is covered with forests sheltering herds of reindeer, roe deer, deer, and moose. The most populated area of the county is the traditional district of Innherred, which runs along the western side of the Trondheimsfjord. Much of the county's agriculture is located here. Crops include barley, oats, potatoes, vegetables, and wheat. Fertile agricultural lowlands on the northeastern shore of the Trondheimsfjord and in the Namdalen valley in the traditional district of Namdalen produce grain as well. Some inhabited islands lie within the Trondheimsfjord, including Ytterøy, which has a large population of roe deer.

Røyrvik, a municipality within the traditional district of Namdalen, is noted for the effort in recent years of some goat farmers to revive the practice of making coffee cheese (*kaffeost*). It is an unsalted white goat cheese, which is dried, smoked, or fried to conserve it. It was a common practice in the mountainous regions from Røros in Sør-Trøndelag to Finnmark county in northern Norway for hikers and workers to add *kaffeost* to their coffee for an energy boost. *Kaffeost* adds little weight to the backpack or work sack, and shavings of the cheese readily melt in the hot coffee. In central Norway, coffee is also paired with moonshine. The result is called *karsk*.

A two-dish meal common to central Norway offers *rømmegrøt,* or sour-cream porridge, as the first course. The second course is *grautpinn,* a plate of cured meat. Another regional dish is *kleppsuppe,* a milk soup with dumplings made from eggs, sugar, milk, and wheat flour.

Preparations representative of the county of Sør-Trøndelag are a curry-flavored, creamy fish soup with bacon, onion, potatoes, and tomatoes from

Rørosfe, or black-sided *Trønder og Nordland,* a breed of cow with black spots on a white background. The animal typically has black color around its eyes, ears, and nose, and a large patch of black on at least one of its sides. Photograph courtesy of Tom Gustavsen.

the municipality of Selbu (*fiskesuppe fra Selbu*); onion and leek soup (*løk- og purresuppe*); and boiled, salted fish balls from the island of Frøya (*saltfiskballer fra Frøya*). Pieces of brown goat cheese are in the center of the balls, which are made of fish, raw and cooked potatoes, cream, and syrup. Boiled potatoes, mashed rutabagas, and salt pork accompany the dish. *Trondhjemssuppe* is a sweet-and-sour milk soup made with rice, raisins, currant or raspberry juice, sugar, and cream or sour cream. The soup, attributed to the city and municipality of Trondheim, is served hot.

Among the many varieties of soft flatbread (*lefse*) prepared in Sør-Trøndelag is *lefse fra Oppdal*, a specialty of the municipality of Oppdal. It is made with milk and a mixture of wheat, rye, and barley flours. One side of the *lefse* is fried; the other is spread with a mixture of egg, buttermilk, and sugar. It is returned to the griddle, spread side up, and fried until the spread is dry. Before the *lefse* is served, it is softened by sprinkling some water on the spread side and that side is then buttered and dusted with cinnamon and sugar. Two circles of *lefse* are sandwiched together, spread sides touching, and cut into wedges.

A well-known specialty of Nord-Trøndelag is a soup-like dish of lamb, lamb meatballs, and carrots in hot broth called *Inherredsodd*. The ingredients are cooked and served separately, so it is a *sodd* rather than a soup. Diners assemble the dish at the table and enjoy boiled potatoes on the side. Another *sodd* preparation is a specialty of the municipality of Grong. *Elgsodd fra Grong* contains small chunks of boiled moose (*elg*) with chopped carrots and rutabagas. *Elgsodd* may also have small meatballs. Dumplings made from barley flour and potatoes (*Snåsaklubb med flesk og duppe*) have a piece of brown cheese and some syrup tucked inside. This specialty of Snåsa is served with salt pork and brown-cheese sauce.

One of several versions of *lefse* in Nord-Trøndelag is unusual in that it is oven-baked. *Namdalsklenning* is made with wheat and barley flours, and brushed on the top with a mixture of cream and beaten eggs. After the *lefse* is baked, it is softened with water and the bottom side is spread with a mixture of butter, sugar, and cinnamon. Each circle is folded in half, buttered sides touching, and cut into wedges. The wedges are coated with a brown-cheese spread (*Namdalsgomme*) and rolled up like a crescent roll, starting with the wide edge. This intricate variation of *lefse* comes from the traditional district of Namdalen.

A dessert of tarts filled with cloudberry cream is attributed to the municipality of Verdal. The dessert's name derives from the resemblance of the tart shells to monk hats (*munkehatter*). A version of the popular buttery almond "manor cake" (*herregårdskake fra Frosta*) uses grated potatoes instead of flour. It comes from the municipality of Frosta.

Northern Norway (Nord-Norge)

There are three counties in northern Norway: Nordland, Troms, and Finnmark. Northern Norway is a long and comparatively narrow strip of land, for the most part. Its southern boundary begins at about the midpoint of the country. It comprises roughly a third of the total land mass, most of which lies above the Arctic Circle. The population is multicultural and includes Norwegians, indigenous Sámi, Norwegian Finns (Kvens), and Russians. The majority of Sámi people live in Finnmark and the northern part of Troms, although many live in other parts of northern Norway and central Norway. Almost all of northern Norway experiences days of total sunlight in the summer and total darkness in the winter.

Nordland county lies north of central Norway. Its long, jagged coastline has many fjords, skerries, and waterfalls. The county is densely forested. Steep mountains rise at the inland edge of the coastal lowlands and another range, the Kjølen, runs along the border between Norway and Sweden. The climate of Nordland is less harsh than would be expected for the high latitude because the Gulf Stream and its continuation, the North Atlantic Drift, have a moderating influence along the coast. Inland temperatures are colder. Some of the higher mountainous areas are covered with glaciers.

The Lofoten archipelego is separated from the mainland by a stretch of sea called Vestfjord. While Lofoten is known for its extensive herds of sheep, it is more famous for its cod fishery and the production of dried cod (*stokkfisk*). In the nearby archipelago of Vesterålen, arctic char (*ishavsrøye*) are farmed. This quality product is bred according to the fish's natural life cycle and has received Protected Geographical Indication (PGI) status, meaning that its qualities are attributable to its geographical origin. PGI status differs from PDO status in that the entire processing of the product need not occur within the designated area. Other important fish along the coast and in the fjords are coalfish or saithe, haddock, herring, wolffish (*steinbit*), redfish (*uer*), and halibut. Trout and salmon can be fished in many of the rivers, and lobsters are caught off the coast. Whales and seals are also hunted.

Most of the population of northern Norway resides in the coastal lowlands. The people earn their living by fishing and hunting, or by working in the forestry, livestock, and dairy industries. Sheep, goats, and domesticated reindeer are bred in the highlands. The wild sheep (Villsau or Gammel Norsk Sau) is raised in Nordland and elsewhere in northern and western Norway. This small, ancient breed has superb meat, and has been given Slow Food Presidium status to help farmers market their product locally in competition with large, modern breeds. The mountain farming community of Misvær is known for goat herding and a mild, light-yellow, goat's-milk cheese called *Misværost,* which was originally produced there.

Deer and roe deer are found in the lowlands and moose roam the forests of Nordland. Wild blueberries, lingonberries, and cloudberries are delightful supplements to the diet.

Representative dishes of Nordland are saithe soup (*seisuppe*) and a dish of partially dried fish (*boknafisk*), usually cod, which is poached and served with bacon, mashed carrots, and butter sauce. *Boknafisk* is a specialty of Lofoten. Poached fresh cod accompanied by its boiled liver and roe is the popular dish *mølje.* A local variation of soft bread (*møsbrømlefse*) is spread with a melted brown-cheese mixture. Blueberry soup served with a cube of frozen whipped cream (*Vesterålens blåbærsuppe med fløteisterninger*) is attributed to Vesterålens.

North of Nordland lies Troms county, with majestic mountains and waterfalls and a coastline characterized by deep fjords and innumerable islands. Birch and pine forests are common.

Important industries are coastal fisheries and agriculture in the south. A major dairy cooperative has an operation in the village of Storsteinnes in the municipality of Balsfjord near Tromsø city, and is a large producer of Norwegian brown cheese (*brunost*). *Misværost* is now produced here, too. The municipality of Kvæfjord, which includes a fjord of the same name, is famous for its strawberries, and proudly depicts them on its coat of arms. Devotees insist that fruit ripening in the long daylight hours of northern summers, where cooler temperatures prevail, are vastly superior in taste to those grown in warmer climates of Norway.

Kvæfjordkake med vaniljekrem, Norway's national cake, is said to have originated in Kvæfjord about one hundred years ago. It is a layer cake with vanilla cream filling. Each of the rich, buttery cake layers is topped with meringue and almonds before it is baked. The dessert is also called *verdens beste* (the world's best). It is served on special occasions, especially Constitution Day (May 17th). The island of Senja is known for the *gulløye* potato, a small tuber with light-yellow flesh and red eyes. It has received PGI status. Senja also is the place to partake of the traditional dish of boiled or fried redfish heads (*uershode*). A hole is poked in the head and the juices are slurped out. Seven heads per serving! The cultivation of an old variety of yellow turnip, *Målselvnepe,* is associated with the municipality of Malselv. Local farmers bred the turnip in the mid-1800s for its ability to grow in the long daylight hours of the short summer. Any new crop was a significant plus for a climate that limits the variety of produce that can be grown. *Målselvnepe* has been added to Slow Food's Ark of Taste to ensure its preservation.

The city of Trømso, the largest city in northern Norway, is located on an island connected to the mainland by a bridge and tunnel. Trømso is home to the Mack Brewery, which was established in 1877. Locals especially enjoy Mackøl with seagull eggs (*måsegg*) from the colonies found along northern Norway's coast. Typically the eggs are eaten hard-boiled, often with Norwegian caviar.

Regional culinary specialties of Troms include a preparation of fish in yeast bread (*fisk i gjærbrød*), cured redfish (*spekeuer*), and cod "tongues" in wine sauce (*torsketunger i vinsaus*). A local strawberry dessert (*jordbærdessert*) is a delicious combination of strawberries in whipped egg white and sweetened cream. Specialties of Tromsø include seal stew (*selgryte*); Barents ham (*Barentsskinke*), a dish of salted and dried seal meat; and a creamy soup with kelp and shellfish (*tang- og skalldyrsuppe fra Tromsø*).

The largest and least-populated county in Norway is Finnmark, which lies at the extreme northeast end of the country. It shares a border with Finland and Russia, and its rugged coastline has many fjords and islands. The western part of the county is generally more mountainous, with glaciers in some areas. In the interior is a large plateau, Finnmarksvidda, which accounts for about a third of the county's area and is home to thousands of reindeer herded by indigenous Sámi. The plateau also has the coldest winters in Norway.

Most of the population lives in the coastal area where the climate is milder, and fishing is the primary livelihood. The red king crab (*kongekrabbe*), which the Russians introduced to the Barents Sea near the Norwegian border at Murmanskfjord in the 1960s, spread west

Hard-boiled seagull eggs (*måsegg*), a specialty of northern Norway.

into Norwegian waters. This delicacy is commercially exploited, and savvy tour companies offer king crab safaris, especially near Norway's easternmost fjord, Varangerfjord. You may dive for your own crab or have someone else catch one for your dinner. Varanger is also know for its gourmet lamb from free-range highland sheep.

Halibut soup with seagull eggs (*kveitesuppe med måsegg*), a specialty of the town and municipality of Vardø, is a typical Finnmark dish. Also typical is a round, flat sour bread (*surbrød*) with crushed caraway seeds. Traditionally, holes were made in the center of the bread so the loaves could be hung on rods near the ceiling to dry. Sámi contributions to the arctic menu include the traditional reindeer stew (*bidos*) with carrots, potatoes, and onions, which is served on special occasions, particularly weddings; hunter's soup (*Finnmarksviddas jegersuppe*) with hare, bacon, cabbage, and carrots; and another reindeer stew (*viltgryte*), this one containing shaved reindeer meat (*finnbiff*), mushrooms, and bacon in a sour cream and brown goat cheese sauce flavored with juniper berries. The stew is also called simply *finnbiff*.

The small volcanic island of Jan Mayan in the North Atlantic Ocean is uninhabited except for a handful of people running a meteorological station and a NATO radio navigation system. The archipelago of Svalbard is the northernmost part of Norway, situated halfway between the mainland and the North Pole. It borders on the Arctic Ocean in the north, the Norwegian Sea in the south, the Greenland Sea in the west, and the Barents Sea in the east. The Global Seed Vault project to conserve the world's food supply is located here. Started in 2008, the vault stores seeds from global seed collections to protect against their loss due to natural disasters or war.

Tastes of Norway

You are heartily encouraged to prepare some of these recipes before you begin your travels. This is a wonderful and immediately rewarding way to preview the cuisine of Norway. The recipe collection includes both traditional and "new Norwegian" preparations. Today, many chefs are devising dishes that showcase Norwegian ingredients in an innovative way, and several of these chefs have won top awards in national and international competitions for their contemporary creations.

Most of the special Norwegian ingredients necessary for these recipes are available in the United States (see *Resources, p. 75*). Satisfactory substitutes are given for those that are unavailable.

BEVERAGE

Rabarbradrikk

Rhubarb drink. Serves 4–5.

The recipe for this refreshing drink was provided by Bjorg Harman, who lives in the village of Gransherad in southern Norway. She is a retired assistant professor of home economics at Telemark University College, Faculty of Arts, Folk Culture and Teacher Education, and is the author of several books on home economics.

1½ POUNDS FRESH RHUBARB, WASHED AND CUT INTO ½-INCH SLICES

9½ CUPS WATER

⅔ CUP SUGAR

2 TABLESPOONS LEMON JUICE, FRESHLY SQUEEZED

5 STRAWBERRIES, THINLY SLICED

Add rhubarb to water and boil 5–6 minutes. Strain juice through a cheesecloth-lined strainer into a bowl. Discard rhubarb. Add sugar and lemon juice to rhubarb juice, stirring well to dissolve the sugar. Chill juice. Add some strawberry slices to each glass before serving. Leftover juice can be refrigerated for a couple of days or frozen.

45

APPETIZER

Gravlaks med Sennepssaus

Cured salmon with mustard sauce. Serves 3–4.
This recipe comes from Robert Ottesen, Executive Chef at Sjohuset Skagen in Stavanger in western Norway. The waterfront restaurant occupies a historic warehouse building and serves delicious Norwegian and international dishes.

1 POUND BONED, CENTER-CUT SALMON FILLET WITH SKIN

2 TABLESPOONS SALT

1 TABLESPOON SUGAR

2 TABLESPOONS COGNAC

2 TABLESPOONS CHOPPED DILL (FRESH OR DRIED)

Mustard sauce

½ CUP MAYONNAISE

1 TABLESPOON DRY SHERRY

2 TEASPOONS SUGAR

¼ TEASPOON SALT

¾ TEASPOON DRIED DILL

1 TEASPOON FINELY MINCED CAPERS

1 TEASPOON FINELY MINCED GHERKIN

1 TEASPOON FINELY MINCED ONION

2 TEASPOONS FINELY MINCED HARD-BOILED EGG

2 TEASPOONS DIJON MUSTARD

2 TEASPOONS WHITE VINEGAR

1 TABLESPOON COLD WATER

To prepare the fish, wash fillet in cold water and dry with paper towels. Slice off fat, if any, on the belly side of the fish. Cut fillet in half crosswise and place both pieces in a small glass or ceramic dish, skin side down. The depth of the dish should be about the same as the combined thickness of the fillets. Mix salt and sugar, and rub the mixture onto the flesh side of each piece. Sprinkle cognac evenly over the flesh and coat surface with dill. Lay one half on top of the other, flesh sides touching, and cover the dish with plastic wrap so that it seals the dish but is not taut. To provide pressure, place a heavy plate that is a little larger than the fish on top. After the fillets have been refrigerated for 3 days, separate them and baste the flesh sides with marinade that has accumulated in the dish. Place the fillets together again as before, and turn the fish upside down. Baste with marinade. Cover the dish with plastic wrap and replace the heavy plate. Refrigerate for 2 more days. Separate the fillets and scrape away the coating of dill with a knife. Dry fillets with paper towels. With the skin side down, thinly slice the fillets on a diagonal, starting from the thinnest end. Discard skin.

To make the mustard sauce, mix the ingredients together by hand, not by machine. If the sauce is too thick, add more water. Adjust the taste to your preference.

To serve, place sliced salmon on plates along with individual bowls of mustard sauce. Chef Ottesen serves this dish with slices of hearty rye bread and garnishes the plates with a few lettuce leaves, a sprig of dill, and some cherry tomatoes cut in half. See color photo insert, p. 4.

SALAD

Lokal Skinke med Salad og Fersk Ost

Local ham with salad and fresh cheese. Serves 4.

This recipe was provided by Kristoffer Hovland, executive chef for over 15 years at the historic Fossheim Turisthotell in Lom in western Norway. Chef Hovland was on the Norwegian National Cooking Team for several years and has won many cooking awards. He was named Best Chef in Norway in 2004.

24 THIN SLICES CURED *SPEKESKINKE* (SALTED AND DRIED HAM)*

2 SMALL RED ONIONS, THINLY SLICED AND SEPARATED INTO RINGS

2 RED RADISHES, THINLY SLICED

2 OUNCES MIXED SALAD GREENS, TORN INTO PIECES

   Cheese balls

8 OUNCES FRESH, SOFT GOAT CHEESE

¼ CUP MINCED PARSLEY

1 TEASPOON DRIED TARRAGON, CRUMBLED

1 TEASPOON LEMON ZEST

1 TEASPOON SALT

1 TEASPOON PEPPER

2 SMALL CLOVES GARLIC, CUT INTO SMALL PIECES

1 TABLESPOON BREAD CRUMBS

   Vinaigrette

1½ TABLESPOONS MUSCATEL VINEGAR

⅓ CUP OLIVE OIL

SALT AND PEPPER TO TASTE

   Sauce

1 TEASPOON CHOPPED DRIED APRICOTS

[Lokal Skinke med Salad og Fersk Ost, *continued*]

    1 TEASPOON RAISINS

    1 TEASPOON DRIED LINGONBERRIES†

    1 TEASPOON WALNUT PIECES

    2 TABLESPOONS HONEY

    2 TABLESPOONS MUSCATEL VINEGAR

    CHIVES FOR GARNISH, CUT INTO ABOUT 3-INCH LENGTHS

Place six slices of ham on each of four large plates. Divide the onion rings, radish slices, and mixed greens into four portions and sprinkle on top of the ham on each plate.

To make cheese balls, roll the cheese into 1" balls (makes about 16 balls). Add the remaining cheese ball ingredients to a food processor and blend well. Roll cheese balls in herb mixture until evenly coated. Arrange four cheese balls on each plate.

To make vinaigrette, blend together vinegar, olive oil, salt, and pepper. Drizzle some vinaigrette over each salad.

To make sauce, warm fruits and nuts in honey over low heat. Add vinegar and stir well. Spoon some sauce over each salad. Serve garnished with chives.

*Many local varieties of *spekeskinke* exist in Norway. See *Resources,* p. 75, for sources. Proscuitto or similarly cured ham obtained from your local farmers' market can be substituted for *spekeskinke.*

†Dried cranberries can be substituted for dried lingonberries.

See color photo insert, p. 1, and front cover for photos of this salad.

BREAD

Engjalandsbrødet

Bread from Engjaland with rolled oats and dried herbs. Makes 2 loaves.

The recipe for this hearty bread was provided by Aud Walaker Hutchinson, an experienced a la carte chef, whose main interest now is cooking outdoors with organic foods. As a member of Vossahuldrene (The Voss Nymphs), Aud is involved with farm tourism in the municipality of Voss in western Norway, where she provides cultural activities and rural accommodation for travelers on her farm.

    4¼ CUPS SKIM MILK

    1 OUNCE ACTIVE DRY YEAST

    3 TABLESPOONS SOYBEAN OIL*

    2 TABLESPOONS HONEY

    1½ TEASPOONS SALT

5 CUPS (14 OUNCES) ROLLED OATS

3 CUPS (14 OUNCES) WHOLE-WHEAT FLOUR

4 CUPS (14 OUNCES) WHITE FLOUR

1 TABLESPOON DRIED HERBS (CHOOSE YOUR OWN FAVORITES)

WATER OR BEATEN EGG FOR COATING

Warm milk to 100°F and pour into a large bowl. Stir in yeast and let soften. Blend in oil, honey, and salt. Gradually stir in oats, wheat and white flours, and herbs. Add more white flour if necessary. Knead the dough on a floured board until it is supple, but not too firm, about 10 minutes. Then knead it further in a food mixer with a bread hook (5–10 minutes) or by hand (about 15 minutes). Place dough in a large bowl and cover it with plastic wrap. Top with a kitchen towel and let dough rise for about 40 minutes. Cut dough into two pieces and form two loaves. Place in lightly oiled 9¼ × 5¼ × 2½" non-stick loaf pans. Let dough rise again under a towel for 30–45 minutes. Brush the surface of the dough with lukewarm water or beaten egg, and sprinkle some rolled oats on it. Bake on the lowest oven rack at 400°F for 30 minutes. Then reduce the heat to 350°F and bake another 35–45 minutes.

*Other vegetable oils such as canola oil may be substituted for soybean oil.

PORRIDGE

Rømmegrøt

Sour cream porridge. Serves 4.

This rich porridge traditionally is served on special occasions, particularly for weddings. The recipe comes from Eli Skjervheim, one of five farm women comprising the Vossahuldrene (The Voss Nymphs), who live in the municipality of Voss in western Norway. The group offers nature-based cultural experiences, often with a food focus. Eli's farm has nurse cows of a rare, native-Norwegian breed called Western Norwegian Fjord cattle, characterized by short legs and small bones.

2⅛ CUPS HEAVY CREAM

2⅛ CUPS BUTTERMILK

1 EGG, BEATEN

⅝ CUP CAKE FLOUR

Topping

CINNAMON

SUGAR

RAISINS

[Rømmegrøt, *continued*]
Combine cream and buttermilk in a medium saucepan. Add egg and cook over medium heat until the mixture boils, stirring frequently. Reduce heat to medium low. While stirring, gradually sift in flour to prevent lumps from forming. A hand-held sieve works well; it can be gently shaken to release flour into the pan while stirring the mixture with the other hand. The porridge will thicken, but continue to simmer until the butterfat separates out and floats over the surface. Stir vigorously to prevent the mixture from browning on the bottom of the pan. The entire cooking process takes about 30 minutes. Serve hot with a sprinkling of cinnamon, sugar, and raisins.

SOUPS

Ertersuppe

Pea soup. Serves 3–4.

This recipe comes from Inge Johnsen, originally from Bjugn, who is co-owner, manager, and chef of Sans & Samling Lian Restaurant in Trondheim in central Norway. Actually a complex of many restaurants, Sans & Samling-Lian serves Norwegian and international cuisine. Chef Johnsen works closely with the older generation of home cooks to help preserve traditional Norwegian recipes.

According to Chef Johnsen, this soup is served with salted meat and usually is eaten on Fat Tuesday, the spirited celebration on the last day before the Catholic observance of Lent. It is also served with pancakes for dinner or as an evening dish on festive occasions.

8 OUNCES YELLOW SPLIT PEAS

5 OUNCES LEAN SALT PORK SIDE

4½ CUPS WATER

1 MEDIUM ONION, CHOPPED

3 MEDIUM CARROTS, PEELED AND SLICED

2 STALKS CELERY, SLICED

2½ CUPS VEGETABLE BROTH

1 TEASPOON DRIED THYME

SALT AND PEPPER TO TASTE

Soak peas in an excess of water overnight. Discard water and rinse peas. Gently boil them together with the pork side in 4½ cups water, stirring occasionally. Skim off scum that forms. After 30 minutes, remove the pork, cut it into small pieces and set it aside. Continue boiling peas for another 30 minutes with occasional stirring, adding a little water if necessary. Add onion, carrots, celery, and broth, and gently boil 30–45 minutes longer, stirring occasionally. Toward the end of the cooking time, add thyme, salt and pepper to taste, and the pieces of pork.

Betasuppe

Meat and vegetable soup. Serves 6.
Randi Engelsen Eide contributed the recipe for this delicious soup of sausage, smoked meat, and root vegetables. The dish is typical of the inland region of western Norway. Randi is one of five women comprising the Vossahuldrene (The Voss Nymphs). All of them farm in the municipality of Voss in western Norway and offer travelers a variety of cultural experiences, including an understanding of the local food. Randi and her family run Sivle, an organic and ecological farm. They grow vegetables and berries, and raise sheep and horses. Dishes prepared from their farm-grown food are served to guests in a traditional 14th-century timber house, or outdoors in combination with a hiking tour.

1¼ POUNDS SMOKED LAMB SHOULDER STEAK*

1¼ POUNDS SMOKED PORK HOCK

10 CUPS COLD WATER

1 POUND NORWEGIAN SAUSAGE (*VOSSAKORV*)†

³⁄₄ POUND CARROTS, PEELED AND SLICED

³⁄₄ POUND RUTABAGA, PEELED AND SLICED

¼ POUND LEEK, SLICED

1 POUND BOILED POTATOES, PEELED

Boil the lamb and pork hock in water in a large pot for 2½ hours, or until the meat loosens from the bones. Remove meat from pot and let it cool a bit before cutting it into pieces. Cut sausage into 2" pieces and add to the meat broth, along with the vegetables (the potatoes will have been boiled separately) and pieces of boiled meat. Add more water if necessary to cover, or if the broth is too salty. Boil for an additional 30 minutes. Serve the meat and vegetables on a large platter; serve the potatoes and broth in separate bowls. *Betasuppe* is typically served with homemade flatbread (*lefse*).

*Unsmoked lamb shoulder steak may be substituted.

†*Vossakorv* is a regional smoked sausage product from the municipality of Voss, which contains beef, lamb, and pork. *Vossakorv* is hard to find in the United States. Substitute a smoked sausage, preferably made with all three meats.

See color photo insert, p. 8.

Main Dishes

Persillebakt Kveite på Risotto av Byggryn

Parsley-baked halibut served on barley risotto. Serves 4.
Chef Heine Grov provided this recipe with Italian overtones from his cookbook *Det Jærski Kjøkken* (The Jæren Kitchen), written with Målfrid Snørteland. He has been

[Persillebakt Kveite på Risotto av Byggryn, *continued*]
a chef at several restaurants and hotels since he was 21 years old. Chef Grov favors the cuisine of the Jæren region of western Norway where he was born.

Risotto

1 TABLESPOON OLIVE OIL

1 SHALLOT, FINELY CHOPPED

1 CUP BARLEY, SOAKED IN WATER FOR AT LEAST 12 HOURS

1 CLOVE GARLIC, MINCED

2–2½ CUPS CHICKEN STOCK

2 TABLESPOONS FINELY GRATED PARMESAN CHEESE

2 TABLESPOONS BUTTER

SALT AND PEPPER TO TASTE

Fish

5 TABLESPOONS BUTTER

½ CUP FINELY CHOPPED PARSLEY

1 CLOVE GARLIC, MINCED

1¾-POUND FILLET OF HALIBUT

To prepare the risotto, heat olive oil in a medium-size frying pan. Add shallot and fry over medium heat until translucent. Add barley and minced garlic, and stir well. Add chicken stock, beginning with ½ cup, and stir constantly while cooking. When barley has absorbed the stock, add another ½ cup stock and continue to stir. Repeat adding more stock and cooking while stirring until the barley is tender but slightly firm to the bite, about 40 minutes. The mixture should not be runny. Mix in Parmesan cheese and butter, then salt and pepper to taste. Set aside and keep warm.

To prepare the fish, melt half of the butter. Put melted butter, parsley, and garlic into a food processor. Mix well until the paste is bright green. Add the remaining (unmelted) butter and mix well. Evenly spread the paste on the halibut fillet and cut fillet into four portions. Bake in preheated oven at 350°F for 20–25 minutes, or until done. Fish should be flaky and white, not translucent. Do not overcook. To serve, place each piece of fish on a bed of risotto. The chef suggests serving the dish with boiled fresh vegetables such as carrots.

Kamskjell "Lyon"

Scallops "Lyon." Serves 4.

The recipe for this "New Norwegian" dish was contributed by Chef Geir Skeie, winner of the prestigious Bocuse d'Or competition in 2009 in Lyon, France. This recipe was inspired by the competition's winning dish, which is in his cookbook,

Geir Skeie, World Cooking Champion: A Taste Journey from Childhood to Bocuse d'Or. Chef Skeie is chef and owner of Brygga 11, a restaurant located in Sandefjord in eastern Norway, about an hour's drive from Oslo.

8 LARGE SHRIMP*

1¼ CUPS WATER FOR STOCK

1 TABLESPOON CHOPPED ONION

1 TABLESPOON CHOPPED CELERY

¾ CUP CREAM

2 TEASPOONS LEMON JUICE

PINCH OF LEMON ZEST

SALT AND PEPPER TO TASTE

1 SHALLOT, THINLY SLICED

2 TABLESPOONS BUTTER

1⅓ CUPS FROZEN PEAS

2–3 TABLESPOONS CHICKEN STOCK

1–2 TABLESPOONS SOFTENED BUTTER

1 SMALL SWEET POTATO, WASHED, PEELED, AND THINLY SLICED

1 TABLESPOON CANOLA OIL

4 LARGE FRESH SCALLOPS

1–2 TABLESPOONS BUTTER

SALT AND PEPPER TO TASTE

⅓ CUP FRESH PEAS

SALT AND PEPPER TO TASTE

4 POACHED QUAIL EGGS (OPTIONAL)

PEA SPROUTS (OPTIONAL)

To prepare shrimp, shrimp stock, and shrimp foam, peel and devein shrimp. Save shells. Boil shrimp for a few minutes until they turn pink. Drain and set aside. Add the shells to water in a small saucepan, along with the onion and celery, and boil for 10 minutes. Strain stock and cool to room temperature. Add cream to ¾ cup cooled stock in a small saucepan and simmer for 10 minutes. Stir in lemon juice and zest, and salt and pepper to taste. Foam mixture with a hand mixer before serving.

To prepare pea purée, sauté the shallot in butter in a small saucepan until transparent. Add frozen peas and chicken stock and boil, covered, for 3 minutes. Add a little more stock, if necessary. Drain liquid and put peas in a food processor with the softened butter. Blend to a smooth purée. Add some stock if necessary. Set aside and keep warm.

[Kamskjell "Lyon," *continued*]
To cook the sweet potato, boil in lightly salted water until just tender, about 2 minutes. Drain and place on an oiled baking sheet. Grill at 450°F for about 5 minutes. Set aside and keep warm.
To cook scallops, heat a small frying pan until it is smoking. Add oil. Fry scallops over high heat until they are golden, about 3 minutes. Remove the pan from the heat and add butter. Turn the scallops over, sprinkle with salt and pepper, and spoon some of the melting butter over them. Heat scallops for a few minutes more if they are not done. Do not overcook.
To prepare the garnish of fresh peas, boil peas for 2 minutes. Drain and cool in ice water. Squeeze the peas out of their skins. Discard skins, and season peas with salt and pepper. Before garnishing the dish, warm fresh peas, together with the shrimp, in a little butter.
To serve, place a dollop of puréed peas in the center of individual plates. Arrange some sweet potato slices over the purée and spoon foam around this mound of vegetables. Garnish the foam with two shrimp and a handful of peas. Place a poached quail egg on the potatoes, if desired. Top with some pea sprouts.
*Chef Skeie uses smoked shrimp in his recipe. He smokes the shrimp whole, then makes shrimp stock using the shells. If you have a home smoker, smoke the shrimp according to the instructions provided.

Innherredsodd

Soup-like dish of lamb, lamb meatballs, and carrots. Serves 4.

This recipe, a specialty of the Innherred region in the county of Nord-Trøndelag in central Norway, was provided by Gunhild Vevik, who comes from Byneset, the countryside outside Trondheim. Gunhild has been in the tourism business for over 20 years, and currently is Project Manager for Region Stavanger BA, the local tourist board in the Stavanger area. This soup-like dish of lamb (small pieces of meat and meatballs), potatoes, and carrots is called *sodd* rather than *suppe* because the ingredients are cooked separately.

Lamb

1 POUND BONELESS LAMB SHOULDER ROAST

7 CUPS SALTED WATER

6 PEPPERCORNS

¼ TEASPOON COARSELY CHOPPED FRESH GINGER

2 TABLESPOONS CHOPPED LEEK

1 BAY LEAF

Meatballs

½ POUND GROUND LAMB

1½ TEASPOONS SALT

½ TEASPOON GROUND GINGER

½ TEASPOON GROUND NUTMEG

PEPPER TO TASTE

1 TABLESPOON POTATO FLOUR

⅔ CUP WHIPPING CREAM

Vegetables

1 OUNCE JULIENNED CARROTS

8 SMALL, WHOLE POTATOES, BOILED

FRESH PARSLEY FOR GARNISH

Boil meat in salted water with peppercorns, ginger, leek, and bay leaf. Skim off any scum that forms. Boil until meat is tender, adding more water if necessary. Remove from heat and cut meat into small cubes. Set aside and keep warm. Reserve broth. To make meatballs, mix ground lamb with salt, ginger, nutmeg and pepper until well-blended. Mix in flour. Add cream, working it into the mixture. Form small balls about the size of a cherry tomato. Recipe makes about 22 balls. Bring broth to a boil and add meatballs. Gently boil for about 5 minutes, or until done. Remove with slotted spoon and set aside. Boil carrots for 5 minutes, remove with slotted spoon and set aside.

To serve, place meat and meatballs together in a bowl and add some hot broth. Top with carrots. Potatoes garnished with parsley are served in a separate dish.

Prinsefisk: Dampet Torskefilet på Hvitvinsaus, med Hummer og Asparges

Fish for a prince: steamed cod fillets in white wine sauce, with lobster and asparagus. Serves 4.

The recipe for this classic dish was provided by Eric Saudan, owner of several fine restaurants in Bergen in western Norway. It is a dish served at Bryggen Tracteursted, his restaurant located in the innermost part of the Hanseatic wharf—Bryggen— which is one of UNESCO's World Heritage Sites.

Sauce

2 SHALLOTS, FINELY CHOPPED

2 TABLESPOONS BUTTER

¼ CUP DRY WHITE WINE*

½ CUP FISH STOCK, WARMED

2 TABLESPOONS FLOUR

1 EGG YOLK

[Prinsefisk: Dampet Torskefilet på Hvitvinsaus, med Hummer og Asparges, *continued*]

1 CUP CREAM

SALT AND WHITE PEPPER TO TASTE

Fish

1½-POUND COD FILLET, WITH SKIN REMOVED

2–3 CUPS FISH STOCK

JUICE FROM ½ LEMON

SALT AND PEPPER TO TASTE

Accompaniments

16 FRESH ASPARAGUS SPEARS

2 TEASPOONS SUGAR

4 SMALL LOBSTER TAILS, BOILED

To make the sauce, fry shallots in a (medium) saucepan over medium heat in butter until light brown. Add wine and reduce to about 2 tablespoons, stirring constantly. Add stock and reduce to about 2 tablespoons, stirring frequently. Blend in flour and stir well. The mixture will thicken rapidly. Remove from burner. Whisk together egg yolk and cream. Slowly add to flour mixture, blending well after each addition. Return pan to stove and cook over low heat to thicken sauce. For a thinner sauce add more warmed fish stock. Season with salt and pepper, and set aside.

To prepare fish, cut fillet into four portions and steam over stock (or salted water), using a fish steamer. Alternatively, construct a steamer by placing a colander on top of a large sauce pot of boiling stock. Place fish in colander and cover with a pan lid smaller than the sauce pot so the lid will rest in the colander just above the fish. Steam fish for three minutes, or until just tender. Place fish on a baking tray and sprinkle with lemon juice, and salt and pepper to taste. Bake in preheated oven at 350°F for 10–15 minutes, or until fish is flaky and white, not translucent.

Add asparagus to about 2 cups boiling water with sugar, and cook about 3 minutes. Do not add salt while cooking or the asparagus will lose its fresh green color.

To serve, place some sauce on each plate, and arrange four asparagus spears, side-by-side, on the sauce. Place fish over the asparagus and top with a small lobster tail.

*Dry sherry can be substituted for dry white wine.

See color photo insert, p. 8.

Blåskjellsuppe med Safran og Karri

Mussel soup with saffron and curry. Serves 2–3.

This recipe was contributed by Daniel Olsen, head chef since 2008 at the Enhjørningen Fiskerestaurant in western Norway, a popular fish and seafood restaurant on Bryggen, Bergen's traditional wharf. The restaurant is housed in a building dating to the early Middle Ages.

¼ TEASPOON FRESH BASIL, CHOPPED

¼ TEASPOON FRESH DILL, CHOPPED

¼ TEASPOON FRESH CHIVES, CHOPPED

¼ TEASPOON FRESH ROSEMARY, CHOPPED

¼ TEASPOON FRESH THYME

¼ CUP SOFTENED BUTTER

1 SHALLOT, FINELY CHOPPED

1 CLOVE GARLIC, FINELY CHOPPED

1 TABLESPOON BUTTER

¼ TEASPOON CURRY POWDER*

PINCH OF SAFFRON

¾ CUP WHITE WINE

2 POUNDS LIVE MUSSELS

1⅔ CUPS CREAM

SALT AND PEPPER TO TASTE

Add herbs to butter and mix well. Set herbed butter aside. Fry shallot and garlic in 1 tablespoon butter (not herbed) over medium heat until soft. Stir in curry and saffron. Blend in wine and bring to a boil. Add mussels and cook until the shells open fully, about 3–5 minutes. Add a little water if necessary. Mix in cream and herbed butter, and blend well. Boil for an additional 2–3 minutes. Do not overcook. Add salt and pepper to taste.

*Chef Olsen uses a commercial curry powder rather than making his own blend. See color photo insert, p. 2.

Ferskt Kjøtt og Suppe

Fresh meat and soup. Serves 4.

This recipe was provided by chef Knut Renslemo, Nesbyen, who is now retired. Chef Renslemo is from Gol in the district of Hallingdal, and began his culinary career in the Norwegian navy. He was a chef in Oslo for many years, and most recently was the chef and owner of Lunchbaren in Nesbyen. This dish of meat boiled with vegetables doubles as two courses: a vegetable soup followed by a main dish of sliced meat topped with sweet-sour sauce and served with some of the same vegetables that are in the soup. A side dish of boiled potatoes accompanies the main dish.

[Ferskt Kjøtt og Suppe, *continued*]

    10 CUPS COLD WATER

    2½ POUNDS BEEF CHUCK ROAST

    1 TEASPOON BEEF BOUILLON POWDER

    6 PEPPERCORNS

    1 MEDIUM PARSLEY ROOT, CHOPPED

    ¼-INCH SLICE OF CELERIAC, CHOPPED

    ½ MEDIUM LEEK, INCLUDING 1–2 INCHES OF THE GREEN STALK, CHOPPED

    1–2 MEDIUM CARROTS, CHOPPED

    ½ HEAD GREEN CABBAGE, CHOPPED

    CHOPPED PARSLEY FOR GARNISH

    Sweet-sour sauce

    2 TABLESPOONS BUTTER

    1 MEDIUM ONION, CHOPPED

    2 TABLESPOONS FLOUR

    1¼–1⅔ CUPS BEEF BROTH (COOKING BROTH)

    2 TEASPOONS VINEGAR

    2 TEASPOONS SUGAR

    ½ CUP HEAVY CREAM

    SALT TO TASTE

    Potatoes

    8 SMALL WHOLE POTATOES, PEELED AND BOILED

    CHOPPED PARSLEY FOR GARNISH

Put water and meat in a large pot. Bring water to boil and remove scum from the surface. When no more scum forms, add bouillon and peppercorns. Boil gently for 1–1½ hours. Add parsley root, celeriac, leek, carrots, and cabbage and boil 15 minutes more. Remove meat and cut into serving slices. Keep warm for the second course. Set aside enough broth for the sweet-sour sauce. Spoon some of the remaining broth into bowls along with some of the boiled vegetables. Serve very hot, topped with chopped parsley.

To make the sweet-sour sauce, melt butter over medium-low heat. Add onion and cook until transparent. Mix in flour. Slowly blend in broth. Let boil for a few minutes. Add vinegar and sugar, and when well-mixed, stir in cream and heat through. Add salt to taste, and more sugar or vinegar if desired. Top beef slices with sweet-sour sauce and serve with soup vegetables and boiled potatoes garnished with chopped parsley. See color photo insert, p. 6.

Fjellørret fra Simadalen med Urtesmør og Lun Potet og Eplesalat

Mountain trout from Simadalen, with herbed butter and warm potato-and-apple salad.
Serves 2.

This recipe was provided by Nils Averå, head chef at the historic Fleischer's Hotel located in Voss in western Norway. Chef Averå comes from Askøy near Bergen. Note: the herbed butter needs to be sliced when cold, so it should be made ahead and refrigerated.

Herbed butter

½ CUP SOFTENED BUTTER

1 CLOVE GARLIC, FINELY CHOPPED

2 TEASPOONS MUSTARD

1 TABLESPOON LEMON JUICE

1 TABLESPOON WORCESTERSHIRE SAUCE

½ TEASPOON TABASCO SAUCE

2 TEASPOONS CHOPPED FRESH PARSLEY

1 TEASPOON CHOPPED FRESH MARJORAM

1 TEASPOON CHOPPED FRESH OREGANO

½ TEASPOON CHOPPED FRESH THYME

SALT AND WHITE PEPPER TO TASTE

Potato and apple salad

5–6 TABLESPOONS MELTED BUTTER

5–6 TABLESPOONS VEGETABLE OIL

3 TABLESPOONS CHOPPED SCALLIONS

1 CUP BOILED, CUBED, UNPEELED NEW POTATOES

½ CUP CUBED, UNPEELED SWEET APPLE

Trout

2 TROUT FILLETS WITH SKIN, 6 OUNCES EACH*

SALT AND PEPPER TO TASTE

BUTTER AND VEGETABLE OIL FOR FRYING, IN EQUAL PORTIONS

2 LEMON SLICES, ABOUT ¼-INCH THICK

SMALL BUNCH WATERCRESS

Blend together the eleven ingredients to make herbed butter. Place mixture on a piece of foil and roll into a cylinder about 2" wide. Refrigerate in the foil until firm. Cut into ¼" slices and keep cold until needed.

[Fjellørret fra Simadalen med Urtesmør og Lun Potet og Eplesalat, *continued*]
Mix together butter and oil. Use a little of this mixture to fry scallions over medium heat until soft. Add potato and apple and continue to fry until warmed thoroughly. Set aside and keep warm. Season fish with salt and pepper. Fry over medium heat, skin side down, in 3–4 tablespoons of the butter and oil mixture for about 5 minutes. Turn fish over and fry until flesh is flaky and no longer translucent, about 3–4 minutes. Serve fish, skin side up, on a bed of the potato and apple mixture. Place a slice of lemon and a slice of herbed butter on the fish. Top with some watercress and serve.
*Rainbow trout can be substituted for mountain trout.
See color photo insert, p. 5.

Kokt Laks

Poached salmon. Serves 2.
Ole-Erik Holmen-Løkken, Executive Chef at To Rom og Kjokken restaurant in Trondheim in central Norway, contributed this recipe. He is from the village of Sander in the eastern part of Norway and has been in the restaurant business since the age of sixteen. In 2001 he won the Norwegian Chefs Championship.
Chef Holmen-Løkken frequently cooks fish and meat using the sous-vide ("under vacuum") method of cooking. This involves vacuum-sealing foods in plastic bags and cooking them in water at precise temperatures in immersion circulators below the boiling point for an extended period of time. Fish cooked this way remains moist and juicy, and tough meats become quite tender. Since vacuum cooking is uncommon outside the restaurant setting, Chef Holmen-Løkken has also provided an alternative cooking method—poaching in cooking oil—to achieve a similar result in the home kitchen. Note: The cucumber garnish, sour cream emulsion, and brine for the fish need to made ahead and chilled.

Cucumber garnish

½ CUP CIDER VINEGAR

½ CUP SUPERFINE SUGAR

½ CUP WATER

1 SMALL CUCUMBER, PEELED AND CUT INTO ¼-INCH SLICES

SALT AND PEPPER TO TASTE

Sour cream emulsion

¼ CUP HEAVY CREAM

⅔ CUP NORWEGIAN SOUR CREAM (RØMME)*

Brine for fish

2 CUPS WATER

2 TABLESPOONS BROWN SUGAR, PACKED

1 SCANT TABLESPOON COARSE SEA SALT

THYME TO TASTE

1 SPRIG WILD GARLIC†

Salmon

2 SALMON FILLETS, 7–8 OUNCES EACH, WITH SKIN REMOVED

2 CUPS OLIVE OIL

1 CUP CANOLA OIL

1 SPRIG WILD GARLIC†

1 SPRIG TARRAGON

Caviar garnish

¾ OUNCE SALMON CAVIAR

1 TABLESPOON FINELY CHOPPED SHALLOTS

1 TABLESPOON FINELY CHOPPED CHIVES

To make cucumber garnish, bring vinegar, sugar, and water to a boil. Refrigerate until chilled. Put cucumber slices in the chilled pickle brine for 30 minutes. Drain briefly on paper towels and season with salt and pepper. Refrigerate until needed.

To make sour cream emulsion, mix cream and sour cream in a small saucepan and carefully warm it over low heat with constant stirring until well-blended. Refrigerate until needed.

To make brine for fish, mix together water, sugar, salt, thyme, and wild garlic, and bring to a boil, stirring occasionally to dissolve sugar and salt. Remove pan from heat and pass brine through a fine mesh strainer. Refrigerate brine until completely cold. Place salmon in a dish and cover with chilled brine. After 30 minutes, remove salmon from dish and pat away excess brine with paper towels.

To cook salmon by the sous-vide method, vacuum seal the fillets in plastic bags and cook at 133°F in an immersion circulator for 12 minutes. To poach salmon on the stovetop in oil, heat the oils with the wild garlic and tarragon on medium-low in a medium-size frying pan. [Note: For stove-top poaching, Chef Holmen-Løkken suggests heating the oil to 133°F, and poaching the fish until its internal temperature reaches 108°F. With the laser thermometer we used, we were not confident that we could differentiate between the temperature of the oil and the internal temperature of the fish, so we heated the oil to 200°F, a temperature frequently used to poach fish.] When the temperature reaches 200°F, turn heat to low and add fish to pan. The oil should completely cover the fish. Cook 6–7 minutes, or until done. Fish should be opaque, not translucent.

To make caviar garnish, mix caviar, shallot, and chives. Top each fish fillet with a spoonful of the caviar garnish just before serving. Swirl some sour cream emulsion alongside the fish and artfully arrange a few cucumber slices on the plate.

[Kokt Laks, *continued*]
*Crème fraîche can be substituted for Norwegian sour cream.
†One sliced garlic clove can be substituted for wild garlic.
See color photo insert, p. 5.

Reinsdyrfilet Fylt med Geitost

Fillet of reindeer stuffed with brown cheese. Serves 2.
This recipe showcases the delicious pairing of game with brown cheese from goat's milk whey (*geitost*). It includes a sauce made with wild berries, considered an excellent complement to game dishes. The recipe was provided by Eric Saudan, owner of Bryggen Tracteursted in western Norway. His restaurant on the historic Hanseatic wharf in Bergen features a menu that combines local and Hanseatic food traditions. Bergen was a member of the Hanseatic League's international trading empire from the 14th to the 16th centuries.

> HANDFUL OF SMALL PORTOBELLO MUSHROOMS
>
> BUTTER FOR FRYING
>
> SALT AND PEPPER TO TASTE
>
> 2 REINDEER FILLETS, ABOUT 6 OUNCES EACH*
>
> 1 OUNCE BROWN CHEESE (*GEITOST*), SOFTENED†
>
> *Game sauce*
>
> 2 CUPS GAME STOCK††
>
> ½–⅔ CUP HEAVY CREAM
>
> ¼ CUP SOUR CREAM
>
> 2 TEASPOONS LINGONBERRIES OR LINGONBERRY SAUCE†
>
> 2 TEASPOONS RED CURRANTS
>
> 2 TABLESPOONS ROWENBERRY JELLY†
>
> 1 OUNCE BROWN CHEESE (*GEITOST*), CUT IN SMALL PIECES
>
> ½ TEASPOON PINK PEPPERCORNS, CRUSHED WELL
>
> ½ TEASPOON DRIED JUNIPER BERRIES, CRUSHED WELL
>
> *Caramel sauce*
>
> 3½ TABLESPOONS SUGAR
>
> ½ CUP HEAVY CREAM
>
> 4 WHOLE CHESTNUTS

Potato purée

2–3 MEDIUM POTATOES, BOILED WITHOUT SALT, THEN PEELED

SOFTENED BUTTER

CREAM

SALT AND PEPPER TO TASTE

MUSCAT WINE TO TASTE

Preheat oven to 350°F. Fry the mushrooms in a little butter, and season with salt and pepper. Set aside and keep warm.

To make a hole in the fillets for the cheese filling, pierce meat with a paring knife in the center of one end, and carefully push knife through to the other end. Hint: it is easier to center the slit if the fillets are gently squeezed to make them rounder. Roll cheese into a cylinder twice the length of an individual fillet and about ½" in diameter. Cut rolled cheese in half. Squeeze each fillet as before, this time to open the slit. Insert a piece of rolled cheese, which will be firm enough to handle despite being softened. Bake fillets, uncovered, for 6 minutes on each side. Let rest 5 minutes before slicing. The cheese should be somewhat runny.

To make the game sauce, boil stock to reduce the volume by two thirds. Add remaining ingredients and cook over medium heat to thicken, about 30 minutes. The cheese should be completely melted. If some small pieces of cheese remain unmelted, press them against the side of the pan with a spoon.

To make the caramel sauce, melt sugar in a small saucepan until caramelized. Blend in cream. Add chestnuts and bring sauce to a boil.

To make potato purée, mash boiled potatoes by hand. Add butter and cream to taste, and blend well. Add salt, pepper, and wine to taste.

To serve, fan out slices of fillet on a mound of potato purée. Top with some game sauce. On the side, place a small amount of caramel sauce with chestnuts.

*Fillet from deer, red deer, or reindeer can be used. See p. 76 of *Resources* for sources of farm-raised red deer and reindeer meat.

†Available in large grocery stores. See *Resources,* p. 75, for online suppliers of Norwegian food products.

††Lamb stock can be substituted.

Sommerlig Kveite fra Kjeurda i Jøsenfjorden

Summer halibut from Kjeurda in Jøsen Fjord. Serves 4.

Frode Selvaag, Executive Chef at the Spa-Hotell Velvære in Hjelmeland in western Norway, provided this recipe for halibut in a light mustard sauce. He serves the dish with new cabbage, asparagus, pickled red onions, and carrots cooked in orange juice. According to Chef Selvaag, this dish is the one most closely associated with him. He and his staff take pride in providing their guests local foods.

[Sommerlig Kveite fra Kjeurda i Jøsenfjorden, *continued*]

1¾-POUND HALIBUT FILLET, WITH SKIN REMOVED

1 TABLESPOON SALT

1½ TEASPOONS SUGAR

Butter-steamed green asparagus and new cabbage

12 STALKS ASPARAGUS, TRIMMED

½ HEAD OF NEW CABBAGE, CUT INTO ½-INCH STRIPS*

1¾ OUNCES BUTTER

½ CUP WATER

SALT TO TASTE

PINCH OF CAYENNE PEPPER

Carrots cooked with orange juice

4 MEDIUM-SIZE CARROTS, PEELED

2 CUPS ORANGE JUICE

1 PIECE OF STAR ANISE

4 PEPPERCORNS

1 BAY LEAF

SCANT ¼ CUP SUGAR

SALT TO TASTE

Pickled red onions

8 SMALL RED ONIONS

¾ CUP RED WINE VINEGAR

¾ CUP WATER

1 TABLESPOON BROWN SUGAR

1 TABLESPOON BUTTER

SALT TO TASTE

Light mustard sauce

¾ CUP WHITE WINE

⅓ CUP WHITE WINE VINEGAR

3½ TABLESPOONS COLD, UNSALTED BUTTER, CUT INTO ½-INCH CUBES

1 TEASPOON COARSE DIJON MUSTARD

1 TEASPOON SMOOTH MUSTARD

1 TEASPOON SUGAR

¾ CUP LIGHTLY WHISKED WHIPPING CREAM

2 TEASPOONS FINELY CHOPPED CHIVES

Fish

2–3 TEASPOONS SUNFLOWER OIL

2 TEASPOONS UNSALTED BUTTER

2 CLOVES OF GARLIC, SLICED

½ TEASPOON TARRAGON

Cut fillet into four equal portions, and rub each with salt and sugar. Set aside for 1 hour before cooking.

Melt butter in water over medium heat, and add salt, cayenne pepper, asparagus, and cabbage. Cook, covered, for about 4 minutes. The cabbage should be crisp and green, not overcooked.

To prepare carrots, parboil for 3 minutes in well-salted, vigorously boiling water. Drain carrots and return to the pot. Add orange juice, spices, and sugar. Salt to taste. Cook over low heat, covered, until the carrots are tender, about 15 minutes. Remove the carrots from the pot and keep warm. Reduce the remaining juice to a syrup by simmering, uncovered, about 25 minutes on medium-low heat. Before serving, slice carrots in half lengthwise and warm them in syrup.

To prepare onions, peel and slice off the bottoms, but leave the tops intact. Mix together vinegar, water, and sugar in a small pan. Place onions upright in pan and bring to a boil over medium heat. Then reduce heat to medium-low and cook about 15 minutes. Remove onions and set aside. Reduce liquid in pan to a syrup over low heat, about 10 minutes, stirring more frequently at the end. Blend in butter and salt to taste. Set aside. Before serving, warm onions in syrup.

To make the mustard sauce, reduce the wine and wine vinegar down to about ½ cup over medium heat. Vigorously whisk in the cold butter and let mixture boil, continuing to whisk for about 1 minute. Add mustards and sugar, and boil another 30 seconds with vigorous whisking. Set aside. Before serving, add the cream and chives, and warm briefly over medium heat. Adjust the taste with salt, sugar, or mustard, if needed.

To fry the halibut fillets, heat a non-stick frying pan over high heat. Add oil and let it smoke a little. Place fillets in pan and fry until golden brown, about 2 minutes. Turn fillets over and add butter, garlic, and tarragon. Reduce heat to medium. Fry for another 2 minutes while basting with the melted butter mixture. Be careful not to overfry the fillets; the fish easily becomes dry from overcooking. Remove fillets from pan to a plate to rest for a few minutes. Serve fish topped with mustard sauce, and arrange vegetables on the plate around it.

*New cabbage (*nykål*) is a small, oval-shaped spring cabbage. A similarly shaped variety of early cabbage called Caraflex can be found in local farmers' markets in the United States, but head cabbage may be substituted if necessary.

Får-i-kål

Lamb and cabbage stew. Serves 5–6.

Most Norwegians consider *får-i-kål* the national dish of Norway. Anne-Grethe and Svein Aanestad, who live in Heddel, near Notodden in southern Norway, contributed their family recipe for this savory stew. It is enjoyed in autumn—especially on national *får-i-kål* day—the last Thursday of September. Plain boiled potatoes typically accompany the stew. The Aanestads are good friends who are passionate about cooking Norwegian food and sharing this enthusiam with others. It was a pleasure to learn more about the cuisine of Norway in their kitchen.

3 POUNDS LAMB (RIBS AND SHOULDER, WITH BONES AND FAT)

2–3 TEASPOONS SEA SALT

1 HEAD CABBAGE, CUT INTO ¼-INCH SLICES

12 CURLS OF MARGARINE, ABOUT 1 TEASPOON EACH

3 TABLESPOONS WHEAT FLOUR

2 TEASPOONS WHOLE PEPPERCORNS

Cut meat into serving-size pieces. Divide meat and other ingredients roughly in half, except for the sea salt, which is to be divided into four parts. The ingredients are placed in a wide, heavy pot in a specific order and the process is repeated to make a second layer. Put meat at the bottom and sprinkle it with sea salt. Next add cabbage and place curls of margarine on top. Sprinkle flour evenly over the surface. Scatter peppercorns over the flour and finish with more sea salt. Repeat with the remaining portions of the ingredients to form the second layer. Fill pot with water to about 1½ inches below the top of the second layer. Bring to a boil and simmer about 2 hours or until the meat is tender. Serve piping hot.
See color photo insert, p. 8.

Ovnsbakt Steinbit med Sjampinjongsaus og Gulrotpuré

Oven-baked arctic catfish with mushroom sauce and carrot purée. Ratatouille accompanies this dish. Serves 2.

Daniel Olsen, Executive Chef at the Enhjørningen Fiskerestaurant in Bergen in western Norway, provided the recipe for this dish. Chef Olsen began his career in the food and hotel industry in his hometown of Åsane, near Bergen. The arctic catfish used in this recipe is also known as wolffish. This fish does not taste like channel catfish, a different species found in the United States.

2 ARCTIC CATFISH FILLETS, 7 OUNCES EACH, WITH SKIN REMOVED*

SOY SAUCE FOR MARINATING

FLOUR FOR COATING FISH

1–2 TABLESPOONS SOFT BUTTER

PINCH EACH OF FRESH PARSLEY, MARJORAM, THYME, AND ROSEMARY

SALT AND PEPPER TO TASTE

Mushroom sauce

1 SHALLOT, CHOPPED

¼ POUND SLICED MUSHROOMS

2 SMALL, WHOLE MUSHROOMS

2–3 TABLESPOONS BUTTER

1 TABLESPOON COGNAC

1–1½ TABLESPOONS SOY SAUCE

1½ CUPS CREAM

SALT AND PEPPER TO TASTE

Ratatouille

½ SMALL ZUCCHINI, CHOPPED

½ GREEN BELL PEPPER, DESEEDED AND CHOPPED

1 SMALL ONION, CHOPPED

1 SMALL, MILD CHILE PEPPER, CHOPPED

1 SMALL CLOVE GARLIC, CHOPPED

1 SMALL TOMATO, SKINNED, DESEEDED, AND CHOPPED

1–2 TABLESPOONS CANOLA OIL

4 TABLESPOONS TOMATO PURÉE

PINCH EACH OF FRESH BASIL, ROSEMARY, AND THYME

SALT AND PEPPER TO TASTE

⅛ TABLESPOON SUGAR, OR TO TASTE

Carrot purée

6 OUNCES CARROTS, CHOPPED

1–2 TABLESPOONS BUTTER

1 TEASPOON CHOPPED CHIVES

SALT AND PEPPER TO TASTE

Garnish

2 SLICES BACON, FRIED

ARUGULA OR WATERCRESS SPRIGS

Preheat oven to 375°F.

Marinate fish in soy sauce for 2 minutes. Pat dry and flour the better-looking side.

[Ovnsbakt Steinbit med Sjampinjongsaus og Gulrotpuré, *continued*]
Fry, floured-side down, in a little butter over medium-high heat for 30 seconds.
Transfer fish to a baking dish, floured-side up. Blend together 1–2 tablespoons soft
butter, herbs, salt, and pepper, and spread mixture on fish. Bake fish uncovered for
10–12 minutes, or until done. Fish should be flaky and white, not translucent.
To make mushroom sauce, fry shallot and mushrooms in butter over medium heat.
Remove whole mushrooms and set aside for garnish on ratatouille. Add cognac, soy
sauce, and cream, and gently boil for 2–3 minutes. Season to taste with salt and
pepper.
To make ratatouille, fry zucchini, pepper, onion, chile pepper, garlic, and tomato in
oil until soft. Add tomato purée, herbs, salt, and pepper. Fry until thoroughly
warmed. Add sugar to taste.
To make carrot purée, simmer carrots until soft. Purée with butter in a food
processor. Add chives, and salt and pepper to taste.
To serve, place fish to one side of plate and spoon some mushroom sauce over it.
Top fish with two half slices of bacon and some arugula or watercress sprigs. On
the rest of the plate, artfully arrange a small mound of carrot purée and a small
mound of ratatouille topped with a whole mushroom.
*Cod, haddock, or turbot may be substituted for arctic catfish.

Sprøstekt Lyr med Saltbakte Røbeter

Crispy fried pollack served with salt-baked beets. Serves 2.
The recipe for this dish was provided by Hanne Frosta, who has been a chef for
over 25 years. Currently she is chef and owner of Hanne på Høyden, an innovative
restaurant in Bergen in western Norway. Chef Frosta's kitchen is defined by
Norwegian tradition and culture, but with a modern twist. Ingredients are obtained
from local organic farms.

COARSE SEA SALT

2 SMALL, UNPEELED BEETS

2 SMALL, UNPEELED NEW POTATOES, ABOUT 5 OUNCES EACH

7 OUNCES KALE

2 7-OUNCE POLLACK FILLETS WITH SKIN*

FINE SEA SALT

CANOLA OIL FOR FRYING

BUTTER FOR HEATING VEGETABLES

2 TABLESPOONS UNSALTED BUTTER

PINCH OF CARAWAY SEEDS

1 TABLESPOON FINELY CHOPPED CHIVES

Cover the bottom of a small oven-proof casserole with coarse sea salt. Place beets on top of the salt and bake at 275°F for 3–4 hours, or until done. To shorten the cooking time, beets may be baked at 350°F for about 2 hours. Cool beets, peel, and set aside. Boil potatoes until done. Slice and set aside. Remove kale from stalks. Quickly blanch leaves and set aside. Sprinkle both sides of the fish with fine sea salt. Using enough oil so that the fish does not stick to the pan, fry over medium to medium-high heat, skin side down, until skin is crispy. The fish should be flaky without having to turn it over to cook the other side. Heat beets, potatoes, and kale in a little butter in separate pans until thoroughly warm. Brown 2 tablespoons unsalted butter in a small pan over medium heat. Add caraway, chives, and fine sea salt to taste. To serve, make a bed of potatoes and cover them with some buttery kale. Place fish on top with crispy skin side up and lay a beet to the side. Pour the savory browned butter sauce on top of the fish.

*If fresh pollack is unavailable, use a firm, white-fleshed fish such as halibut, sea bream, haddock, or cod.

Reinsdyrfilet med Fløtesaus

Fillet of reindeer with cream sauce. Serves 4.

This delectable game recipe comes from Walter Kieliger, Executive Chef since 2005 at the historic Frognerseteren in southern Norway, a magnificent and ornate 19th-century wooden mountain lodge outside Oslo. Swiss-born and educated, Chef Kieliger has worked as chef and executive chef for a variety of cruise lines and international hotels. He moved to Norway in 1973, and since 1992 has been running his own restaurants.

Cream sauce

2 SMALL SHALLOTS, CHOPPED

1 TABLESPOON BUTTER

1 TABLESPOON RED-CURRANT JELLY

½ CUP PORT WINE

¾ CUP HEAVY CREAM

2 CUPS MEAT STOCK

1¼ OUNCES BROWN GOAT CHEESE (*GEITOST*), CUT IN SMALL PIECES*

½ CUP SOUR CREAM

SALT AND PEPPER TO TASTE

Meat

7 OUNCES SMALL MUSHROOM CAPS

1–2 TABLESPOONS BUTTER

[Reinsdyrfilet med Fløtesaus, *continued*]

1¼ POUNDS FILLET OF REINDEER, WITH FAT REMOVED†

2–3 TABLESPOONS BUTTER

Preheat oven to 175°F. To prepare sauce, glaze the shallots in butter in a small frying pan over medium heat. Mix in jelly and cook until mixture begins to brown slightly. Add wine and cook until liquid is almost gone, stirring frequently. Add cream and stock, and simmer for about 1 hour over low heat, stirring occasionally. Strain sauce and return to a saucepan. Stir in cheese and sour cream, and cook over low heat until well-blended. Season with salt and pepper. While the sauce is simmering, sauté mushrooms in butter. Set aside and keep warm. To cook the fillet, melt butter in a frying pan. Add fillet and fry on medium-low heat for about 4 minutes on each side. If deer fillet is substituted for reindeer fillet, cook for about 6 minutes on each side. Complete cooking in the oven for 15 minutes; this will provide a fillet that is cooked medium. Carve the fillet in slices and artfully stack some in the center of individual plates. Surround the slices with sauce and some mushroom caps. Place remaining sauce in a small bowl on the table. Chef Kieliger recommends serving the dish with seasonal vegetables and potato croquettes.

*Brown goat cheese (*geitost*) is available in large grocery stores. See also *Resources,* p. 75, for online suppliers of Norwegian food products.

†Fillet from deer, red deer, or reindeer may be used. See p. 76 of *Resources* for sources of farm-raised red deer and reindeer meat.

See color photo insert, p. 2.

DESSERTS

Rabarbragrøt

Rhubarb fool. Serves 4–6.

The recipe for this simple but lovely dessert porridge was provided by Per Sverre Øvrum, who lives in southern Norway and is a distant cousin of the author's Norwegian-American husband. Per Sverre is a retired teacher and, despite being in his eighties, he still thrives on the great outdoor activities of hiking, biking, and skiing. Fortunately, he is just as happy in his kitchen, cooking and baking Norwegian specialties for his children, grandchildren, and great-grandchildren— and culinary guidebook writers.

3 CUPS RHUBARB, CUT IN ½-INCH SLICES

SCANT CUP SUGAR

3 CUPS WATER

2 TABLESPOONS POTATO STARCH

1 TEASPOON VANILLA

1 DROP RED FOOD COLORING (OPTIONAL)

CREAM OR WHIPPED CREAM

Cover rhubarb with water in a large bowl and soak in the refrigerator for about 24 hours to reduce the acid. Mix sugar and water together in a pan. Drain rhubarb and add to the sugar water. Boil gently until rhubarb softens, stirring occasionally, about 15 minutes. Strain rhubarb and press it with the back of a spoon to release liquid back into the pan. Set rhubarb aside. Remove pan from stove. While stirring continuously, slowly add potato starch to the cooking liquid through a small sieve to help prevent lumps from forming. When all the starch has been added, bring the liquid to a gentle boil over medium heat to thicken. Remove pan from stove and stir in vanilla. Add food coloring if a deeper pink color is desired. Add rhubarb and mix well. Refrigerate before serving with cream or whipped cream.

Karamellpudding

Caramel pudding. Serves 4.

The recipe for this popular Norwegian pudding comes from Randi Øvstebø and Anna Solheim, who created their version of it for the restaurant in Byrkjedalstunet, a picturesque and cozy hotel in Dirdal (Rogaland County) in western Norway. Byrkjedalstunet, owned by Randi and her husband, Daniel, specializes in traditional Norwegian foods using local ingredients. Note: four small loaf pans (5 × 2¾ × 1⅞") will be needed for this recipe.

Caramel

VEGETABLE OIL TO COAT PANS

½ CUP SUGAR

Pudding

3 CUPS MILK

½ CUP SUGAR

1 VANILLA BEAN

8 LARGE EGGS

WHIPPED CREAM FOR DECORATION

4 WHOLE STRAWBERRIES

4 SPRIGS FRESH MINT

Evenly coat loaf pans with a thin film of vegetable oil. Set aside.

To make caramel, heat sugar in a small saucepan over medium heat, stirring constantly. The sugar will liquify and caramelize quickly. When the sugar is a rich brown color and while still hot, rapidly put about one tablespoon of it in each pan.

[Karamellpudding, *continued*]

Using pot holders, tilt pans to evenly coat their bottoms. As the caramel cools it will crack in several places, but these cracks disappear when the pudding is baked. Set pans aside.

Preheat oven to 250°F. To make pudding, mix together milk, sugar, and vanilla bean, and bring to a boil over medium-high heat. Remove milk mixture from the burner and let cool to lukewarm. Remove and discard vanilla bean. Whisk eggs well and add to milk mixture. Pour mixture through a sieve to remove any thickened bits of egg white before evenly distributing the mixture into the loaf pans. Place pans in a 9 × 13" cake pan and put on oven rack. Carefully add water to the larger pan so the bottom two thirds of the loaf pans are submerged. Bake for 1½ hours. Cool to room temperature. Run a sharp knife along the edges of the pudding, down to the bottom of the pan. To unmold, place a serving plate on top of the loaf pan and overturn plate and pan. If the pudding has been refrigerated overnight, it may be necessary to briefly place the loaf pans in some warm to hot water to get them to unmold. Decorate the top of the pudding with some whipped cream, a strawberry, and a sprig of mint.

See front cover for a photo of this dessert.

Vossabia Honningbrød

Vossabia honey bread. Serves many.

The recipe for this nutritious bread, or cake, comes from Renate Lunde, a member of Vossahuldrene (The Voss Nymphs), a group of five farm women in the municipality of Voss in western Norway, who provide nature-based experiences for area visitors. This includes food, cultural activities, art, and accommodation. Renate runs an ecotourism business called Vossabia (the Voss Bee) in connection with her farm and apiary, and has accommodations for guests in comfortable historical houses.

> 1⅔ CUPS HONEY
>
> SCANT ¼ CUP KEFIR (SOUR MILK)*
>
> 3 EGGS, BEATEN
>
> 2 TEASPOONS CINNAMON
>
> 1 TEASPOON POWDERED GINGER
>
> ZEST FROM 1 LEMON
>
> 4½ CUPS RYE FLOUR
>
> 1 TEASPOON BAKING POWDER
>
> BROWN CHEESE (*GEITOST*), OPTIONAL†

Heat oven to 300°F. Warm the honey in a large pan over low heat to make it more fluid. Remove pan from heat. Mix kefir and eggs together, and stir into honey. Add spices and zest, mixing well. Sift together flour and baking powder, and gradually add to mixture in the pan, stirring well after each addition. Lumps that form will break up as more of the flour mixture is vigorously stirred in. Pour batter into a lightly buttered 5¼ × 9¼ × 2½" loaf pan, and bake for 1 hour, or until a toothpick poked into the center of the bread comes out clean. The bread tastes delicious buttered and topped with a slice of brown cheese (*geitost*) made with goat's milk whey.

*Available in large grocery stores and natural food stores.

†Available in large grocery stores. See *Resources,* p. 75, for online suppliers of Norwegian food products.

Honningglaserte Epler

Honey-glazed apples. Serves 2.

Kirsti Indreeide, owner, innkeeper and Head Chef at Petrines Gjestgiveri, contributed the recipe for this simple but scrumptious dessert. Her charming guesthouse in Norddal in central Norway was originally built in 1916 as a home for the elderly on the farm that has been in her family for generations. In 1992 Kirsti converted the building into an inn, where she serves her guests a marvelous variety of regional specialties. It is fitting that Kirsti selected an apple recipe for this guidebook. The daughter of the first Petrine family to own the farm was an amateur horticulturalist who developed the "Petrine apple," a few trees of which still remain on the property.

> 2 TABLESPOONS BUTTER
>
> 2 TABLESPOONS HONEY
>
> 4 TEASPOONS SUGAR
>
> PINCH OF CINNAMON, OR TO TASTE
>
> 2 PEELED APPLES, EACH CUT IN 6 WEDGES
>
> 4 TEASPOONS RAISINS
>
> VANILLA ICE CREAM
>
> *Garnish*
>
> 1 LEMON SLICE CUT IN HALF
>
> CHOCOLATE SYRUP

Mix together butter, honey, sugar, and cinnamon in a small frying pan over medium to medium-low heat. When well-blended, add apples and fry 4–5 minutes, stirring frequently. The apples should be somewhat firm, not mushy. Add raisins and simmer another 1–2 minutes with stirring. Serve on individual plates. Next to the apple mixture place a scoop of ice cream. Garnish with a half slice of lemon

[Honningglaserte Epler, *continued*]
standing upright on the cut edge and leaning against the ice cream. Finish with a drizzle of chocolate around the dessert.

Sjokolade og Myntekake

Mint chocolate cake. Serves many.
This recipe was provided by Valborg Kløve Graue, one of five women in the group called Vossahuldrene (The Voss Nymphs). Each member has a farm in the municipality of Voss in western Norway, and each offers food and cultural experiences for travelers. Valborg has been a farmer and outdoor teacher for 25 years, and currently is a master's degree student in environmental and social action research.

1 STICK PLUS 3 TABLESPOONS BUTTER, SOFTENED

1¼ CUPS BROWN SUGAR, PACKED

3 EGGS

3½ OUNCES DARK CHOCOLATE (70%), FINELY GROUND

1 TEASPOON VANILLA

2–3 TEASPOONS DRIED MINT, FINELY GROUND

1¾ CUPS FLOUR

1 TEASPOON BAKING POWDER

½ TEASPOON SALT, OR TO TASTE

Preheat oven to 350°F. Mix together butter and brown sugar until well-blended. Beat in eggs, one at a time. Stir in chocolate, vanilla, and mint. Sift together flour, baking powder, and salt, and add to the batter. Pour batter into a lightly buttered 4½ × 8 × 2¾" loaf pan and bake on a low oven shelf for 1 hour, or until a toothpick poked into the cake comes out clean.

Resources

Suppliers of Norwegian Food Items

Most of the special ingredients required for the recipes in this book (see *Tastes of Norway,* p. 45) are available in the United States from online suppliers of Norwegian food products. Many of these businesses stock an impressive range of fresh, frozen, cured, smoked, and tinned products: meats and sausages, fish, cheeses, preserves, and baked goods.

Among the larger purveyors of Norwegian food products are:

Willy's Products
954-316-1350
www.willysproducts.com
sales@willysproducts.com

Scandinavian Specialties
877-784-7020
www.scanspecialties.com
info@scanselect.com

Nordic House
800-854-6435
www.nordichouse.com
ordersnordichouse.com

Nordic Delicacies
718-748-1874
www.nordicdeli.com
nordicdeli@aol.com

Kings Norsk Products
303-422-3394
www.kingsnorsk.com
kongeogdronning@comcast.net

Haram-Christensen Corp.
201-507-8544
www.haramchris.com
(wholesaler)

Scandinavian South
941-923-4313
www.scandinavian-south.com

Suppliers of specialty game meats:

Gooch Farms
262-593-5806
goochfarms@hotmail.com
Contact: John Gooch, owner
(Farm-raised European red deer)

J.T. Elk Valley Ranch
715-597-3555
Contact: Jeffry Fritz, Owner
(Farm-raised reindeer and elk)

Specialty cookware items are available from some of the businesses listed on page 75, and from the following companies:

Lefse Time, Inc.
800-687-2058
www.lefsetime.com
info@lefsetime.com

Ingebretsen's
800-279-9333
www.ingebretsens.com
info@ingebretsens.com

Tours and Travel Advice

Norway has an expansive rural tourism program. Ample opportunities exist throughout the country for travelers to stay in rural accomodations, taste traditional regional food on farms, and take part in local activities. A catalog listing food and tourism businesses in rural Norway can be browsed online, or a copy can be ordered from:

Norwegian Rural Tourism & Traditional Food
(011) (47) 22 05 46 40
www.nbg-nett.no
post@nbg-nett.no

The Vossahuldrene (The Voss Nymphs) is a group of five women who farm in Voss in western Norway. They offer travelers a wide range of local cultural and culinary experiences. Some of them provide rural accommodation.

Vossahuldrene
Contact: Valborg Kløve-Graue
v-kloeve@online.no

Some Useful Organizations to Know About

Norwegian Government and Tourism Offices

Royal Norwegian Embassy
2720 34th Street NW
Washington, DC 20008
202-333-6000
www.norway.org/embassy/washington
emb.washington@mfa.no

Royal Norwegian Consulate General
825 Third Avenue, 38th floor
New York, NY 10022
646-430-7500
www.norway.org/embassy/newyork
cg.newyork@mfa.no

Harald Hansen
Information/Public Relations Manager
Innovation Norway Tourism
655 Third Avenue, Suite 1810
New York, NY 10017
212-885-9751
harald.hansen@innovationnorway.no
www.visitnorway.us

International Organizations

Two non-profit, international travel organizations, The Friendship Force and Servas, promote good will and understanding among people of different cultures. These organizations share similar ideals but operate somewhat differently. Friendship Force members travel in groups to host countries. Both itinerary and travel arrangements are made by a member acting as exchange director. These trips combine stays with a host family and group travel within the host country. Servas members travel independently and make their own contacts with fellow members in other countries, choosing hosts with attributes of interest from membership rosters.

For more information about membership in these groups:

Friendship Force International
127 Peachtreet St., Suite 501
Atlanta, GA 30303
404-522-9490
404-688-6148 (fax)
http://thefriendshipforce.org

US SERVAS, Inc.
1125 16th St., Suite 201
Arcata, CA 95521
707-825-1714
info@usservas.org
http://usservas.org

Helpful Phrases

For Use in Restaurants and Food Markets

In the Restaurant

You will find the following Norwegian phrases useful in ordering food, learning more about the dish you ordered, and determining what specialties of a region are available. Each phrase also is written phonetically to help with pronunciation. Syllables in capital letters are accented. Note that when a word ends in "e," that "e" is always pronounced, and it generally sounds like the "e" in "eh." You will find that Norwegians are pleased that you try to speak in Norwegian, even though most of them speak English.

DO YOU HAVE A MENU?	Har du en meny? *Hahr dew ehn meh-NEE?*
MAY I SEE THE MENU?	Kan jeg se på menyen? *Kahn yai say poh meh-NEE-ehn?*
WHAT DO YOU RECOMMEND?	Hva anbefaler du? *Vah AHN-beh-fah-lehr dew?*
DO YOU HAVE . . . HERE? (ADD AN ITEM FROM THE MENU GUIDE OR THE FOODS & FLAVORS GUIDE.)	Har du . . . her? *Hahr dew . . . hehr?*

Helpful Phrases

WHAT IS THE "SPECIAL" FOR TODAY?	Hva er dagens rett?
	Vah ahr DAH-gehns reht?
DO YOU HAVE ANY SPECIAL LOCAL DISHES?	Har du noen lokale retter?
	Hahr dew new-ehn low-KAHL-leh REHT-ehr?
IS THIS DISH SPICY?	Er denne retten sterkt krydret?
	Ahr DEHN-eh REHT-ehn stehrkt KRID-dreht?
I/WE WOULD LIKE TO ORDER . . .	Jeg / Vi vil gjerne bestille . . .
	Yai / Vee vill YEHRN-eh beh-STILL-eh . . .
WHAT ARE THE INGREDIENTS IN THIS DISH?	Hvilke ingredienser er i denne retten?
	VILL-keh in-GREH-dee-EHN-sehr ahr ee DEHN-eh REHT-ehn?
WHAT ARE THE SEASONINGS IN THIS DISH?	Hvilke krydder er i denne retten?
	VILL-keh KRID-dehr ahr ee DEHN-eh REHT-ehn?
THANK YOU VERY MUCH. THE FOOD IS DELICIOUS.	Mange takk. Maten var deilig.
	MAHNG-eh tahk. MAH-ten vahr DAI-lee.

In the Market

The following phrases will help you make purchases and learn more about unfamiliar produce, spices, and herbs.

WHAT ARE THE LOCAL FRUITS AND VEGETABLES?

Hvilke frukter og grønnsaker dyrkes i nærområdet?
VILL-keh FRUHK-tehr oh GREHN-sah-kehr deer-kiss ee NAAR-ohm-ROH-deh?

WHAT IS THAT CALLED?

Hva heter det?
Vah HEH-tehr deh?

DO YOU SELL . . . HERE? (ADD AN ITEM FROM THE FOODS & FLAVORS GUIDE.)

Har du . . . her?
HAHR dew . . . hehr?

MAY I TASTE THIS?

Kan jeg få smake det?
Kahn yai foh SMAH-keh deh?

WHERE CAN I BUY FRESH . . . ?

Hvor kan jeg kjøpe fersk . . . ?
Vor kahn yai HEH-peh fahrshk . . . ?

HOW MUCH IS THIS PER KILOGRAM?

Hva koster det per kilo?
Vah KOH-stehr deh pehr HEE-loh?

I WOULD LIKE TO BUY ¼ KILOGRAM OF THAT.

Jeg vil gjerne ha en kvart kilo av det.
Yai vill YEHRN-eh hah ehn kvahrt HEE-loh ahv deh.

MAY I PHOTOGRAPH THAT?

Kan jeg ta et bilde av det?
Kahn yai tah eht BILL-deh ahv deh?

81

Other Useful Phrases

Sometimes it helps to see in writing a word or phrase that is said to you in Norwegian, because certain letters sound distinctly different in English than in Norwegian. You may be familiar with the word and its Norwegian translation but less familiar with its pronunciation. The following phrase comes in handy if you want to see the word or phrase you are hearing.

PLEASE WRITE IT ON MY PIECE OF PAPER.

Kan du skrive det ned for meg, takk?
Kahn dew SKREEV-eh deh NEHD for mai, tahk?

Interested in bringing home books about Norwegian food?

WHERE CAN I BUY A NORWEGIAN COOKBOOK IN ENGLISH?

Hvor kan jeg kjøpe ei norsk kokebok på engelsk?
Vor kahn yai HEH-peh ai nohrshk KOO-keh-book poh EHNG-ehlsk?

And, of course, the following phrases also are useful to know.

WHERE IS THE RESTROOM?

Hvor er toalettet?
Vor ahr toh-ah-LEH-teh?

MAY I HAVE THE CHECK, PLEASE?

Kan jeg få regningen, takk?
Kahn yai foh RAI-ning-ehn, tahk?

DO YOU ACCEPT CREDIT CARDS?

Tar du kreditkort?
Tahr dew KREH-dit-kohrt?

TOP LEFT Chef Frode Selvaag of Spa-Hotell Velvære, Hjelmeland, with his famous *laks med rømme på ei seng av agurk,* salmon on a bed of cucumbers topped with sour cream. **TOP RIGHT** Inge Johnson of Sans & Samling Lian Restaurant, Trondheim, holds the traditional dish *fersk kjøtt og løksaus,* fresh meat with onion sauce. **LOWER LEFT** *Flesk og duppe,* fried salt pork served with boiled potatoes topped with a sauce made from the pork drippings, made by Bjorg Harman, Gransherad. **BOTTOM** *Lokal skinke med salad og fersk ost,* local ham with salad and fresh cheese, made by Kristoffer Hovland of Fossheim Hotell, Lom.

TOP LEFT *Blåskjellsuppe med safran og karri,* mussel soup with saffron and curry, prepared by chef Daniel Olsen of Enhjørningen Fiskerestaurant, Bergen. **TOP RIGHT** *Krotakaker,* regional soft flatbread (*lefse*) made by Randi Engelsen Eide of the Vossahuldrene, Voss. **MIDDLE** Doughnut (*smultring*) vendor at the Aal outdoor market. **BOTTOM LEFT** *Havregrøt,* oatmeal porridge, made by Aud Walaker Hutchinson of the Vossahuldrene, Voss. **BOTTOM RIGHT** *Reinsdyrfilet med fløtesaus,* fillet of reindeer with cream sauce, prepared by chef Walter Kieliger of Frognerseteren, Oslo.

TOP LEFT Chef Hanne Frosta of Hanne på Høyden, Bergen, holds her popular tomato salad with raspberry sauce, leek, and white goat cheese, *tomat salat med bringebær, purreløk, og hvit geitost.* **TOP RIGHT** Chef Mikael Forselius of Røros Hotell, Røros, with his classic *røye sautert i eplesider på en seng av gulrøtter med mandelpoteter fra Røros,* a fish dish of char cooked in apple cider on a bed of carrots with almond potatoes from Røros. **BOTTOM** Artisanal white and brown goat's milk cheeses from Undredal Stølsysteri, a small dairy cooperative in the village of Undredal.

TOP LEFT Flatbreads and cookies sold at the Aal outdoor market. **TOP RIGHT** Chef Morten Rathe of Rica Nidelven Hotel, Trondheim, offers his signature dish of scallops with a medley of vegetables, *kammuslinger med diverse grønnsaker*. **BOTTOM LEFT** *Variasjon av lokal kje,* a local dish of kid steak and ribs, prepared by chef Maria Berglind of Fretheim Hotel, Flåm. **BOTTOM RIGHT** *Gravlaks med sennepssaus,* cured salmon with mustard sauce, a traditional offering by chef Robert Ottesen of Sjøhuset Skagen, Stavanger.

TOP LEFT *Kokt laks,* poached salmon, prepared by chef Ole-Erik Holmen-Løkken of To Rom og Kjokken, Trondheim. **TOP RIGHT** Reindeer fillet with carrots and cabbage, *reinsdyrfilet med gulrøtter og kål,* prepared by Kirsti Indreeide, owner and chef of Petrines Gjestgiveri, Norddal. **MIDDLE** Tempting fish at the Bergen fish market. **BOTTOM LEFT** Assorted cured meats, *spekemat,* served by chef Robert Ottesen of Sjohuset Skagen, Stavanger. **BOTTOM RIGHT** Mountain trout from Simadalen, with herbed butter and warm potato-and-apple salad, *fjellørret fra Simadalen med urtesmør og lun potet og eplesalat,* prepared by Nils Averå of Fleischer's Hotel, Voss.

TOP LEFT Chef Knut Renslemo from Nesbyen with the soup course from the traditional two-course meal of fresh meat and soup, *ferskt kjøtt og suppe.* **TOP RIGHT** Fried mountain lake trout, *stekt fjellørret,* prepared by chef Hans Tollefsen, Sevletunet. **BOTTOM** Colorful produce section of an outdoor market in Bergen. The selection of fruit includes many imported varieties.

TOP LEFT Kirsti Indreeide, owner and chef of Petrines Gjestgiveri, Norddal, presents her delicious *laksesuppe med kål og gulrøtter,* creamy salmon soup with cabbage and julienned carrots. **TOP RIGHT** Old kitchen utensils, including special rolling pins to make soft flatbread (*lefse),* displayed at Byrkjedalstunet, a hotel in Dirdal. **BOTTOM** Elegant and inviting dining room in the Fleischer's Hotel, Voss.

TOP LEFT *Rømmebrød,* a delicious flatbread containing sour cream, served by chef Knut Renslemo, Nesbyen. **TOP RIGHT** Simmering *dylle,* a regional sweet made from milk and rice, at the Aal outdoor market. **MIDDLE** *Betasuppe,* a rich meat and vegetable soup, prepared by the women of the Vossahuldrene, Voss. **BOTTOM LEFT** *Prinsefisk: dampet torskefilet på hvitvinsaus, med hummer og asparges,* fish for a prince: steamed cod fillets in white wine sauce, with lobster and asparagus, a classic dish served at Bryggen Tracteursted, Bergen. **BOTTOM RIGHT** Norway's national dish, *får-i-kål,* a stew of lamb and cabbage, prepared by Anne-Grethe Aanestad, Heddel.

Menu Guide

This extensive alphabetical listing contains the names of food preparations in Norwegian with English translations to help you order from a menu. The entries—primarily traditional Norwegian dishes—were obtained from a large number of Norwegian and English sources, including cookbooks, restaurant menus, books and articles about Norwegian food, professional chefs, home cooks, and foodies. A few menu entries combining Norwegian and continental elements have also been included in this listing. Norwegian chefs recently have had excellent success in international competitions. Geir Skeie, the latest Norwegian chef to win the prestigious Bocuse d'Or international competition (in 2009), contributed his recipe for Scallops "Lyon" (*Kamsjell "Lyon"*) to our chapter *The Tastes of Norway* (p. 52).

The *Menu Guide* will be useful in any setting where food is offered, not only in restaurants. A rural fair provides an excellent opportunity to sample traditional regional dishes, some of which are sufficiently time-consuming or complicated that restaurants do not feature them. Signs will be posted at the food stalls listing the offerings, so plan to have this guidebook in hand.

The Norwegian alphabet has 29 letters. The three letters that are not in the English alphabet—the vowels **æ, ø,** and **å**—are placed at the end of the Norwegian alphabet. The letters **c, q, w, x,** and **z** are not used in indigenous words, nor do they appear to any great extent in loan words, which usually are spelled using Norwegian phoenetics.

Norwegian *Bokmål* (book language), one of two official forms of written Norwegian, is the language used in this book. Most Norwegians write and publish in *Bokmål*. The other official form, Norwegian *Nynorsk* (new Norwegian), is the official language of serveral counties and municipalities.

It is important to note that the (original) meaning of words may change when the words are joined together as one word. For example, *hvit* means white and *løk* means onion, but together they mean garlic (*hvitløk*).

To understand the old regional references in the names of some of the menu items in this *Guide,* it helps to know about both the traditional districting system of Norway and the modern system of formal administrative units. Traditional districts were based on geographical aspects of the country, such as fjords, valleys, and mountain ranges, and many only partially coincide with the new geographical boundaries established in the early 1900s. At that time Norway was divided into 5 major regions with a total of 19 counties. Each county was further subdivided into municipalities, for a total of 430. (See map, p. 16.) The regions and counties are as follows: Nord-Norge (northern Norway) with 3 counties, Finnmark, Troms, and Nordland; Trøndelag (central Norway) with 2 counties, Nord-Trøndelag and Sør-Trøndelag; Vestlandet (western Norway) with 4 counties, Møre go Romsdal, Sogn og Fjordane, Hordaland, and Rogaland; Sølandet or Agder, (southern Norway) with 2 counties, Vest-Agder and Aust-Agder; and Østlandet (eastern Norway) with 8 counties, Telemark, Buskerud, Hedmark, Oppland, Akershus, Oslo, Vestfold, and Østfold.

The *Menu Guide* includes typical Norwegian dishes as well as dishes that may only be available regionally. Some of the entries in this chapter have comments next to them in the margin. Noteworthy dishes that are popular throughout much of the country are labeled "national favorite" and are not be missed. Classic regional dishes that also are not to be missed are labeled "regional classic." Of course, some regional classics are national favorites as well. Comments on some of our favorites also are included in the margin.

Norwegians dine often, eating as many as six meals a day. Breakfast (*frokost*) is a fairly substantial meal with a wide selection of foods, likely to include crusty bread and rolls, cake, waffles, hard-boiled and cold, scrambled eggs, sliced tomatoes and cucumbers, stewed and fresh fruit, and sometimes porridges such as warm oatmeal (*havregrøt*) sprinkled with raisins or sugar. The choices of toppings or spreads for open-face sandwiches (*smørbrød*) are considerable: jams and jellies, pickled herring, smoked fish, an assortment of cured meat (*spekemat*) and cheeses (*ost*), particularly the lightly caramelized and pleasantly sweet brown cheese made from goat's milk whey (*geitost*). Beverages include coffee, tea, milk, and juice. A light mid-morning snack (*dugurd,* or *kaffe*) might be a pastry with coffee.

Lunch (*lunsj,* or *formiddagsmat*) is taken around noon. It is a lighter meal than breakfast and consists primarily of open-face sandwiches (*smørbrød*) with topping options of cold cuts, cheese, and fish. School children take a packed lunch (*matpakke*) to school since schools in general have no cafeterias providing food for sale. Packing open-face sandwiches in the *matpakke* is somewhat of an art form. The sandwiches are stacked in layers, separated by small rectangular pieces of paper (*mellomleggspapir*). The entire pile is then bundled up with a larger piece of paper (*matpapir*), which serves as a plate when the *matpakke* is opened. Most business people bring a *matpakke* from home as well, even if there is food service at work.

Dinner (*middag*) is the major and only hot meal of the day. Dinnertime ranges from about 3 to 7 PM, but the more usual dining hour is about 5 PM. In rural areas this meal can be as early as noon. Traditional dinner choices are hearty meat (or fish) and potato dishes such as fish balls (*fiskeboller*), meat stew (*lapskaus*), and meatballs (*kjøttkaker*). The accompanying potatoes are almost always boiled. Common vegetable choices are cooked carrots or mashed rutabagas, with plenty of thin, dry flatbread (*flatbrød*) on the side. At any time in the afternoon or early evening there is a pleasant repast of coffee and cakes (*kaffe og kaker*), which is more of a social occasion than a meal. It is enjoyed more frequently on weekends with invited guests. A light evening meal or snack (*aftens,* or *kveldsmat*) is usually eaten between 8 and 9 PM. The selection is somewhat similar to that of breakfast (*frokost*) except for the absence of sweets.

Norwegians typically say "*takk for maten*" at the end of a meal, which means "thanks for the food" in Norwegian. If you have the opportunity to dine in a Norwegian home, it would be a courtesy to remember this.

In restaurants, breakfast is typically available between 7 AM to 10 AM. In some restaurants it is possible to select foods from the breakfast menu until lunchtime. Lunch is available from about 11:30 AM to 2 PM. Dinner is relatively early, around 5 or 6 PM, and earlier in winter. Since a typical work day is over about 3 or 4 PM, the dinner hour conforms somewhat to this schedule. Generally speaking, tips are not expected in restaurants. A service charge of 10% is usually included in the bill.

The sale of alcoholic beverages in restaurants is not restricted. Purchases can be made on Sundays as well.

A word about water: if, from experience, you know you are sensitive to changes in drinking water, your best option is to drink bottled water or canned beverages. It makes sense to err on the safe side, even if the local tap water is judged safe to drink.

The information in this *Menu Guide* should be used in conjunction with the *Foods & Flavors Guide* to explore Norway's menus with confidence. The *Menu Guide* cannot include all dishes that could be offered. The extensive list of translated ingredients in the *Foods & Flavors Guide* is a handy aid to determine what key ingredient distinguishes a particular dish on a menu if it is not included in the *Menu Guide*.

agurksalat cucumber salad.

EXCELLENT **akevitt gravet laks med sennepsaus** salmon marinated in aquavit and served with mustard sauce.

ansjossalat anchovy salad.

appelsinsalat orange salad.

appelsinsyltet gulrot carrots pickled in orange juice.

aprikoskompott apricot compote.

arme riddere "poor knights," a fried dessert of bread soaked in a mixture of egg, sugar, and milk flavored with cinnamon. It is served with jam or red sauce made of red berry juice thickened with cornstarch. Compare with a fancier version of this dessert, *rike riddere,* or "rich knights."

asparges med spekeskinke asparagus with cured ham.

NATIONAL FAVORITE **avkokt torsk** poached or boiled cod.

avlett round, flat, crispy cookie made of barley flour and fried in a special pastry iron (*avlett* iron), which creates a delicate pattern on each side. *Avletter* are especially enjoyed during the Christmas holiday season. They are a regional specialty of Gudbrandsdalen, a valley and traditional district in Oppland county in eastern Norway.

REGIONAL CLASSIC **bacalao** stew of Spanish origin made of dried, salted fish (*klippfisk*), usually cod, with potatoes and tomatoes. It is a specialty of Kristiansund, a city and a municipality in Møre og Romsdal county in western Norway.

NATIONAL FAVORITE **baller** potato dumplings, usually made with grated raw potatoes with a little boiled potato added to help hold the raw potato together. Other names for *baller* are *potetballer, raspeballer, komler (kumler), klubb,* or *klump,* depending on the region of the country.

banankrem creamy dessert of mashed bananas in vanilla-flavored, sweetened whipped cream.

NATIONAL FAVORITE **benløse fugler** stuffed meat rolls made with a mixture of mashed potatoes, ground beef, and ground pork, and traditionally filled with marrow or pork fat flavored with ginger and clove.

REGIONAL CLASSIC **Bergensk fiskesuppe** fish soup made with saithe (a type of cod), carrots, and celery root in a sweet-and-sour broth thickened with cream and egg yolk. The soup typically is served with a sprinkling of cut chives on top. It is a specialty of Bergen, a coastal city in Hordaland county in western Norway.

Bergensk surstek sauerbraten marinated in buttermilk. It is a specialty of Bergen, a coastal city in Hordaland county in western Norway.

Bergenske vannkringler "water-baked" pretzels, which probably were introduced as a food item in Bergen by German merchants living along the wharf during Hanseatic times. The pretzels are boiled in water and then baked. It is a specialty of Bergen, a coastal city in Hordaland county in western Norway.

Berlinerkranser shortbread-like cookies in the shape of a wreath. *Berlinerkranser* are a much-loved traditional Christmas treat. **NATIONAL FAVORITE**

betasuppe meat and vegetable soup. See recipe, p. 51.

bidos reindeer stew, the traditional Sami dish served on special occasions, especially weddings. **REGIONAL CLASSIC**

bifflapskaus beef stew, a variety of *lapskaus,* the salted or fresh meat and root vegetable stew in thick gravy. See *lapskaus.* **NATIONAL FAVORITE**

biskopkake cake made of whipped eggs and sugar, flour, almonds, and raisins. It is a specialty of Vestfold county in eastern Norway. **NATIONAL FAVORITE**

blandaball balls made of ground fish and raw potato, typically with a piece of salt pork in the center.

blodpannekaker pancakes with blood in the batter.

blodpudding med brød blood pudding with bread.

blodpølse fra Torpo i Hallingdal blood and lung sausage. It is a specialty of Torpo, a village in the traditional district of Hallingdal in Buskerud county in eastern Norway.

blomkål med rekesaus cauliflower with shrimp sauce.

blomkålsuppe cauliflower soup.

bløtkake layer cake filled with whipped cream and fruit, and iced with whipped cream. **NATIONAL FAVORITE**

bløtkokt soft-boiled egg.

blåbærgelé gelatin dessert with blueberry juice and white wine.

blåbæris parfait of blueberries and ice cream.

blåskjellsuppe med safran og karri mussel soup with saffron and curry. See recipe, p. 56.

boknafisk dish of partially dried fish (*boknafisk*), usually cod, which is poached and served with bacon, mashed carrots, and butter sauce. It is a specialty of the Lofoten archipelago in northern Norway. **REGIONAL CLASSIC**

brenneslesuppe nettle soup.

bresert lammerull braised lamb roll prepared with boneless side of lamb.

brimsoll broken pieces of flatbread and melted brown goat cheese (*geitost*) topped with butter and sour cream. It is a regional dish of western Norway.

brudlaupskling wedding *lefse*. It is made with rye flour and is fried on one side only. The unfried side is spread with a creamy mixture of cheese, syrup, caramelized sugar, eggs, and flour. Two circles are sandwiched together, spread sides touching, and cut into wedges. It is a version of *lefse* from western Norway.

NATIONAL FAVORITE **brun lapskaus** thick stew of beef, carrots, onions, and potatoes in brown gravy. See *lapskaus*.

brødpudding bread pudding.

byggmelskrumkaker crispy waffle cookies made with barley flour. See *krumkaker*.

byggrynskrem cold dessert porridge made with pearl barley and served with red fruit sauce.

dagens suppe med hjemme baket brød soup of the day with home-baked bread.

GOOD CHOICE **dampet laks med agurksalat og pisket rømme** steamed salmon with cucumber salad and whipped sour cream.

den lille lekre appetizer of small potato pancakes served with smoked salmon and sour cream.

dessertpudding av torskerogn baked rice pudding with cod roe, served cold with a red fruit sauce.

DELICIOUS **dessertsuppe med tyttebær** thickened dessert soup of apples and lingonberries served with whipped cream.

dravle fra Ryfylke curdled whole milk, simmered with cinnamon and mixed with eggs, sour cream, buttermilk, cream, flour, and sugar. This dish comes from Ryfylke, a traditional district in Rogaland county in western Norway.

dravle fra Voss curdled raw whole milk, simmered until golden brown. It is a specialty of the municipality of Voss in Hordaland county in western Norway.

NATIONAL FAVORITE **Dronning Maud's dessert** special-occasion whipped dessert made with egg yolks, sugar, cream, gelatin, and shaved chocolate. Layers of the gelatin mixture alternate with layers of shaved chocolate. A chef in Haugesund, a town in Rogaland county in western Norway, is credited for creating this dessert when Norway's Queen Maud and King Haakon VII visited the town in the 1900s.

eggedosis thick eggnog-like dessert made of whipped egg yolks and powdered sugar. *Eggedosis* is served alone or as a fruit topping, and can be flavored with vanilla or dusted with cocoa powder. It traditionally is eaten on Constitution Day, May 17th. NATIONAL FAVORITE

eggeomelett med spinat omelet with spinach.

eggerøre scrambled eggs.

eggost (eggeost) cheese curds made from a mixture of milk, eggs, sour milk, and sugar. It is eaten with cinnamon and sugar sprinkled on top.

elgkarbonader lean moose patties.

elgkarbonader fra Sør-Trøndelag lean moose patties fried with crushed juniper berries. This preparation is attributed to Sør-Trøndelag county in central Norway. REGIONAL CLASSIC

elgsodd fra Grong soup-like dish of small chunks of boiled moose meat with chopped carrots and rutabagas. *Elgsodd* may also include small meatballs. The dish is a specialty of the municipality of Grong in Nord-Trøndelag county in central Norway. REGIONAL CLASSIC

Engjalandsbrødet bread from Engjaland made with rolled oats and dried herbs. Engjaland is a farm in the municipality of Voss in Hordaland county in western Norway. See recipe, p. 48.

epledessert med karamellsaus apple dessert with caramel sauce.

epleflesk fried salt pork with apples.

eplemos med pepperrot applesauce with horseradish.

eplemunker raised balls of dough, flavored with cardamom and filled with a little applesauce or chopped apple. See *munker*.

epleomelett apple omelet.

eplesild fried fresh herring served with chopped onion and apples. GOOD CHOICE

eplesuppe med einebær apple soup flavored with juniper.

ertekaker pancakes made with pea flour.

ertersuppe pea soup. See recipe, p. 50.

ertestuing stewed peas.

estelumpe small, irregular-shaped pieces of rolled, griddle-fried yeast dough. Usually *estelumpe* is buttered and topped with thin slices of cheese.

falsk skilpaddesuppe mock turtle soup, which contains carrots, celery, and small pieces of boiled meat from calves' heads. Hard-boiled eggs and fish balls usually accompany the dish.

farsert rådyrstek med ovnsstekte rotgrønnsaker stuffed roast of roe deer with roasted root vegetables.

NATIONAL FAVORITE **fattigmann bakkelser** "poor man's cookies," traditional, cardamom-flavored Christmas cookies, which are deep-fried and sprinkled with powdered sugar. To form their characteristic knotted shape, diamond-shaped pieces of rolled dough are slit lengthwise in the center, and one point of the diamond is pulled through the slit.

fattigmanns trøst med hollandsk saus cooked black salsify root with hollandaise sauce.

NATIONAL FAVORITE **fenalår** salted and dried leg of lamb, typically served thinly sliced.

ferskt kjøtt og suppe fresh meat and soup. See recipe, p. 57.

REGIONAL CLASSIC **finnbiff** stew of shaved reindeer meat (*finnbiff*), mushrooms, and bacon in a sour cream and brown goat cheese (*geitost*) sauce flavored with juniper berries. It is a traditional dish of Finnmark county, at the northeast end of Norway, which is home to the Sámi, the indigenous people of Finnmark. The dish is also called *viltgryte*.

REGIONAL CLASSIC **finnmarksviddas jegersuppe** hunter's soup, with hare, bacon, cabbage, and carrots. It is a traditional dish from the high mountain plateau in Finnmark county in the northern most corner of Norway.

fisk i gjærbrød fish in yeast bread. It is a specialty of Troms county in northern Norway.

fisk og kål i gryte one-dish meal of fish, cabbage, and carrots.

NATIONAL FAVORITE **fiskeboller i hvit saus** fish balls in a white sauce.

fiskefarse fra Åsnes baked pudding-like dish of minced fish mixed with flour, milk, and cream. It is a preparation attributed to Åsnes, a municipality in Hedmark county in eastern Norway.

fiskegrateng fish au gratin.

fiskekabaret fish in aspic.

NATIONAL FAVORITE **fiskekaker** fish cakes made of ground fish, chopped onion, and milk or cream. A little flour or potato starch is added to stiffen the mixture, which is formed into patties and fried.

fiskekomle i fiskesuppe fish dumplings in fish soup.

NATIONAL FAVORITE **fiskepudding** fish pudding.

fiskepudding med reker og dill fish pudding with shrimp and dill, thickened with potato flour, rolled into a cylinder, and steamed. The cooked pudding is sliced and fried until browned on both sides.

NATIONAL FAVORITE **fiskesuppe** fish soup.

fiskesuppe fra Selbu curry-flavored, creamy fish soup with bacon, onion, potatoes, and tomatoes. It is attributed to Selbu, a municipality in Sør-Trøndelag county in central Norway.

fjellørret fra Simadalen med urtesmør og lun potet og eplesalat mountain trout from Simadalen, with herbed butter and warm potato-and-apple salad. See recipe, p. 59.

flatbrød thin and crispy griddle-fried flatbread, traditionally made with barley or oat flour, or both, and water. Flatbread accompanies most meals, and today is unlikely to be homemade.   TASTY

flesk og duppe fried salt pork served with boiled potatoes, which are topped with a sauce (*duppe*) made from the pork drippings.

fleskepannekaker pancakes with pieces of fried salt pork in the batter.

flyndre med østerssaus flounder with oyster sauce.

flømri festive, lemon-flavored gelatin dessert with whipped sour cream and powdered sugar, generously mixed with sherry. It is a speciality of Hordaland county in western Norway.

fløtegratinerte poteter scalloped potatoes topped with cheese.

fløterand med friske bær vanilla cream gelatin dessert served with fresh berries.

fløtestuet løk creamed onions.

frikassé av fårekjøtt mutton fricassée.

friske jordbær med vaniljeis fresh strawberries with vanilla ice cream.   NATIONAL FAVORITE

fruktkake fruitcake.

fruktsalat med fløtekaker fruit salad with whipped-cream cake.

fruktsuppe fruit soup.   NATIONAL FAVORITE

fylt and stuffed duck.

fylt hodekål head cabbage stuffed with a minced meat mixture.

fylt reinsdyrhjerte reindeer hearts stuffed with a sautéed mixture of mushrooms, onions, and bits of bacon.

fylt svinekam med sviskesaus pork loin rubbed with ginger and stuffed with prune sauce.

fyrstekake "royalty cake," which is made with a pastry layer topped with rich and chewy almond paste scented with cardamom. A lattice of pastry strips decorates the almond paste layer.   DELICIOUS

får-i-kål lamb and cabbage stew. See recipe, p. 66.   NATIONAL FAVORITE

gammeldags agurksalat sliced cucumber salad prepared the old-fashioned way: salted cucumber slices are pressed to release some of their water before they are mixed with an oil and vinegar dressing.

REGIONAL CLASSIC **gammelsaltet sei** poached salted saithe, a fish in the cod family. Traditionally, the dish is served with potatoes and root vegetables such as carrots, turnips, and rutabagas. It is a regional specialty of Trøndelag (central Norway).

gjeddekabaret pike in aspic.

glasert laks salmon in aspic.

DELICIOUS **gomme** thick pudding made from milk curdled with buttermilk or rennet and boiled for hours until light brown. It is mixed with egg, sugar, flour, and sometimes raisins, and flavored with anise or cinnamon.

REGIONAL CLASSIC **grautpinn** plate of cured meat. *Grautpinn* is enjoyed as part of a two-dish meal in Trøndelag (central Norway). The first course is *rømmegrøt,* or sour cream porridge.

gravet sik cured whitefish.

gravlaks cured salmon.

gravlaks med sennepssaus cured salmon with mustard sauce. See recipe, p. 46.

EXCELLENT **grove medisterkaker med surkål** pork patties with sauerkraut.

grytestek pot roast.

grønn ertestuing creamed green peas.

gul ertesuppe med salt svineknoke yellow pea soup with salted pork leg.

halvgraut "half porridge," an equal mix of sour cream porridge (*rømmegrøt*) and rice porridge (*risgrynsgrøt*).

Hardangerbrød type of patterned *lefse* made from a yeast dough containing wheat or rye flour and sometimes mashed potatoes. See *krotakake.*

harestek med tyttebær hare roast with lingonberries.

POPULAR **hasselbackpoteter** baked potatoes topped with cheese. The dish is made from peeled raw potatoes thinly cut crosswise to within one-half inch from the bottom so the slices remain attached to the base of the potato.

havreflarn thin, oatmeal wafer cookies. Baked *havreflarn* are gently pressed against a rolling pin while still hot to make them curved.

havregrøt oatmeal porridge.

havrekjeks oatmeal cookies.

helgryns byggrøt med aprikos whole-grained barley porridge with apricots.

helkokt ørret poached whole trout.

helstekt gris roasted suckling pig.

herregårdskake fra Frosta "manor cake," a buttery almond cake. NATIONAL FAVORITE
This version contains grated potatoes instead of flour. The cake is attributed to Frosta, a municipality in Nord-Trøndelag county in central Norway.

hitterkake omelet with chives, which is eaten with dried, cured ham. The name of the dish apparently stems from hunters on Hitra Island off the coast of Sør-Trøndelag in central Norway, who found the omelet so easy to make outdoors that it became one of the meals they routinely cooked when hunting.

hjortegryte venison stew.

hjortetakk "hart's (deer's) horns," traditional, ring-shaped cookies NATIONAL FAVORITE
made at Christmastime. Before each cookie is fried, it is snipped at three evenly spaced points on the outside edge of the ring. The points on the ring where the snips were made look a little like hart's horns, or antlers, after the cookies are fried.

hodesylte pickled pig's head meat.

hokkaidosuppe creamy soup made of leeks and a variety of REGIONAL CLASSIC
pumpkin named after the largest Japanese island, Hokkaido. It is a dish from the municipality of Voss in Hordaland county in western Norway.

Holmenkollens eplekake Holmenkollen's pudding-like apple HEAVENLY
cake with a puff pastry crust and a sour cream sauce topping. This cake is a prized specialty of Frognerseteren, a famous restaurant in the small neighborhood northwest of Oslo's city center called Holmenkollen.

honningglaserte epler honey-glazed apples. See recipe, p. 73.

honningkake honey cake.

hummersuppe med tomat lobster and tomato soup.

husets blåskjellsuppe house mussel soup, fresh mussels steamed in white wine with cream flavored with curry and saffron.

hveteboller sweet bread rolls.

hvetekake med syltet ingefær sweet yeast bread with candied ginger.

hvit dame multilayered sponge cake with a filling of strawberry REGIONAL CLASSIC
jam and whipped cream between each layer. Elegant touches include a layer of macaroon with hazelnuts placed near the bottom of the cake and a covering of marzipan over the whipped-cream icing. This special cake comes from Bergen, a coastal city in Hordaland county in western Norway.

høns kokt i vin chicken cooked in wine.

hønsesuppe med byggryn chicken soup with barley.

REGIONAL CLASSIC **Innherredsodd** soup-like dish of lamb, lamb meatballs, and carrots in hot broth. Because the ingredients in this preparation are cooked separately and assembled at the table, the dish is called a *sodd* rather than a *suppe* (soup). The *Innherredsodd* is a specialty of Innherred, a traditional district in central Norway. See recipe, p. 54.

isterklubb dumplings with brown goat's milk cheese (*geitost*) and syrup inside.

REGIONAL CLASSIC **jegergryte** hunter's stew. The version from western Norway contains venison or reindeer, bacon, and prunes.

jordbær med likør strawberries with liqueur.

EXCELLENT **jordbærdessert** strawberry dessert. One version from northern Norway has strawberries in whipped egg white and sweetened cream.

jordeplegrøt potato porridge thickened with barley flour, a specialty of Telemark county in eastern Norway. Also called *potetgrøt*.

Juleboller cardamom-flavored buns.

Julebrød a rich, cardamom-flavored Christmas bread with raisins

NATIONAL FAVORITE and citron. Also called *Julekake*.

Juledagskjøtt breaded veal chops simmered in syrup and sour cream. It is a special Christmas day dish in western Norway.

Julekake a Christmas bread. See *Julebrød*.

Juleøl malty, dark beer brewed only at Christmastime.

kald kjernemelksuppe cold buttermilk soup.

GOOD CHOICE **kaldskål** summer dish of cold yogurt and sweetened whipped cream with chopped almonds or toasted whole oats.

kalvdans og tyttebær velvety pudding made from unpasteurized colostrum milk and lingonberries. The milk is taken from the first or second milking after a cow has given birth.

kalvebrystgryte stew of veal breast.

kalvekjøttkaker veal meatballs.

kamlefse fra Snåsa *lefse* made with potatoes and rye flour, which is baked rather than griddle-fried. After the *lefse* is baked, it is spread with a batter of sweetened eggs, milk, cream, and flour. Characteristic lines on the surface of the batter are made with a brass comb (*kam*) and the *lefse* is baked again. This version of *lefse* is from Snåsa, a municipality in Nord-Trøndelag county in central Norway.

kamskjell "Lyon" scallops "Lyon," named for Lyon, France, the location of the annual Bocuse d'Or international culinary competition. See recipe, p. 52.

kaneleplekake cinnamon apple cake.

kantarellsalat chanterelle salad.

karamellpudding caramel pudding. See recipe, p. 71. DELICIOUS

karbonader fried, lean ground-meat patties. NATIONAL FAVORITE

kardemommeboller cardamom buns.

karrisuppe curry soup.

karvekålsuppe soup made with caraway sprouts.

kjøttkaker med brun saus og stuet kål fried meatballs with brown NATIONAL FAVORITE gravy and creamed cabbage.

kleppsuppe milk soup with dumplings made from a batter of REGIONAL CLASSIC eggs, sugar, milk, and wheat flour. This dish is a specialty of Trøndelag (central Norway).

klinelefse fra Aust-Agder fried potato *lefse* spread with an egg and milk mixture or with unpasteurized milk. The *lefse* is refried to dry the spread. This variety of *lefse* is from Aust-Agder county in southern Norway.

klubb potato dumplings. See *potetballer*. GOOD CHOICE

klubb og duppe potato dumplings with brown goat cheese (*geitost*) sauce. This version is a specialty of Trøndelag (central Norway). NATIONAL FAVORITE

klubben fra Trondheim potato dumplings with some salt pork in the center. It is a specialty of Trondheim in Sør-Trøndelag county in central Norway.

kneipploff multigrain bread.

kokaost fresh cheese molded in a cake pan with a layer of raisins in the center and cinnamon and sugar sprinkled on top.

kokt laks poached or boiled salmon. See recipe, p. 60.

kokt laks med sandefjordsmør poached salmon with Sandefjord NATIONAL FAVORITE butter, the traditional fish sauce containing cream, butter, and chives or parsley. The sauce is named for city of Sandefjord in Vestfold county in eastern Norway.

kokt purre boiled leeks.

kokt røkt kolje poached smoked haddock.

kokt tørrfisk boiled dried cod.

komlastek baked dish of grated potatoes topped with slices of salt pork.

NATIONAL FAVORITE **komler (kumler)** potato dumplings. See *potetballer.*

koppduppe boiled potatoes and curdled milk.

korpsrundstykker hard rolls.

krabbesalat crab salad.

krabbesalat med koriander crab salad with coriander.

NATIONAL FAVORITE **kransekake** ring cake made of ground almonds, sugar, and egg whites. Successively smaller rings of baked dough are stacked on top of each other and held together with icing, producing a cone-shaped cake. *Kransekake* is served at celebrations, including the Christmas holidays.

krokanfromasj mousse made with crushed almond brittle.

krotakake type of patterned *lefse* made from a yeast dough containing wheat or rye flour and sometimes mashed potatoes. A conventional rolling pin is used to make thin circles of dough, which then are scored in perpendicular directions with a special grooved rolling pin (*krotakakekjevle*). This forms a characteristic grid pattern in the dough and prevents the formation of air pockets during frying. Circles of *krotakake* can be dried after frying and stored without refrigeration for later use. They are softened by placing under a stream of tap water and then allowed to rest for about 15 minutes. *Krotakaker* typically are spread with a mixture of butter and sugar, sometimes with whipped cream on top of that, and rolled up. This style of *lefse,* also called *Hardangerbrød,* comes from Hardanger, a traditional district within Hordaland county in western Norway. Sheets of dry *krotakake* are also available commercially.

WONDERFUL **krumkaker** crispy waffle cookies traditionally made during the Christmas season. They are cooked in a special two-sided iron, which forms a design on each side of the cookie. When golden brown on both sides, the cookies are removed from the iron and rolled into tubes or cones. They are eaten plain or filled with whipped cream or other fillings.

kryddersild spiced herring.

krydret hvitost cottage cheese with herbs.

kveite på fat halibut baked in brown sauce.

kveitesodd broth with small pieces of halibut and vegetables.

REGIONAL CLASSIC **kveitesuppe med måsegg** halibut soup with seagull eggs. It is a specialty of Vardø, a town and municipality in Finnmark county in northern Norway.

Kvæfjordkake med vaniljekrem layer cake with vanilla cream filling. Each of the rich, buttery cake layers is topped with meringue and almonds before it is baked. This dessert is said to have originated about one hundred years ago in Kvæfjord, which is both the name of a municipality and a small fjord in Troms county in northern Norway. *Kvaefjordkake,* which has become known as Norway's national cake, is also called *verdens best* (the world's best). It is served on special occasions, especially Constitution Day on May 17th.

kyllingsuppe med pasta chicken soup with noodles.

kålrotstappe mashed rutabagas.

kålruletter med hvit saus stuffed cabbage leaves with white sauce.

lakakurv pickled sausages made with variety meats.

laks kokt i skiver poached salmon slices.

laks og eggerøre smoked salmon and scrambled eggs.

laksekotelett salmon cutlet.

lakserognsalat salmon roe salad.

lakserulader med asparges salmon rolls with asparagus.

lakseruller med pepperrot og eplekrem slices of smoked salmon spread with a mixture of whipped cream, horseradish, and grated apple, and rolled up.

lam med løkstappe lamb with mashed onions.

lammelår i surmelk med potetmos leg of lamb in buttermilk with mashed potatoes.

lammestek slices of roast lamb in gravy.

langpannekake fra Jæren "long pan cake" made with yeast dough and raisins, topped with a mixture of sugar, butter, syrup, and chopped almonds before baking. It is a specialty from Jæren, a traditional district in the country of Rogaland in western Norway.

lapper griddle-fried, cultured-milk pancakes with leavening agent, spread with butter and sugar, jam, or cheese, and folded in half. *Lapper* are called *sveler* in the traditional district of Sunnmøre in Møre og Romsdal county in western Norway. Tiny cultured-milk pancakes are called *skjebladkaker*. See *sveler* and *skjebladkaker*. Also see *pannekaker.*

lapskaus stew of meat (salted or fresh) and root vegetables in thick gravy, an ideal dish for using leftovers. *Lys lapskaus* is a variation without brown gravy and often with salted meat; *brun lapskaus* has brown gravy. Also see *lovløs saltlapskaus.*

NATIONAL FAVORITE **lefse** traditional, soft Norwegian flatbread rolled into thin circles and usually griddle fried. Regional differences include the use of different flours—rye, barley, or wheat, or a combination of the three—with or without mashed potatoes. Some *lefse* are spread with various mixtures, which may or not require additional frying, and can be folded in complex ways.

lefse fra Oppdal variation of a spread *lefse* made from milk and a mixture of wheat, rye, and barley flours. One side is fried; the other is spread with a mixture of eggs, buttermilk, and sugar. The *lefse* is returned to the griddle, spread side up, and fried until the spread is dry. Before the *lefse* is served, it is softened by sprinkling some water on the spread side. The spread side is then buttered and dusted with cinnamon and sugar. Two circles of *lefse* are sandwiched together, spread sides touching, and cut into wedges. This variation is a specialty of the municipality of Sør-Trøndelag, a county in central Norway.

lefse fra Romsdal *lefse* made with potato and cultured milk and spread with a mixture of cream, syrup, and flour. The circle of *lefse* is folded in half, spread sides touching, and cut into wedges. This *lefse* variation comes from Møre og Romsdal county in western Norway.

lefseklining fra Årdal multi-layered *lefse* served in thin strips. It is made from dough containing sour milk and syrup, and after individual circles of *lefse* are fried, they are spread with a mixture of butter, sugar, buttermilk, and cream. The layering is accomplished through an intricate combination of folding portions of a single *lefse* circle on top of itself and stacking specific-shaped pieces from other single *lefse* circles to generate a rectangular *lefse* several layers thick. This variation of *lefse* comes from Årdal, a municipality in the country of Sogn og Fjordane in western Norway.

lekkerbiskener thin, crisp almond cookies.

levergryte med timian liver casserole with thyme.

GOOD CHOICE **leverpostei** liver pâté.

Lierne spesialsalat med varmrøkt sik salad of smoked whitefish with hard-boiled eggs, tomatoes, potatoes, beets, and green olives, served on a bed of lettuce. It is a specialty of Lierne, a municipality of Nord-Trøndelag in central Norway.

REGIONAL CLASSIC **lime-marinert sjørøye med stuet sopp** lime-marinated arctic char with creamed mushrooms. This dish comes from Troms county in northern Norway.

lokal skinke med salad og fersk ost local ham with salad and fresh cheese. See recipe, p. 47.

lomper potato pancakes. Larger *lomper* are used as hot dog buns. See *pølse i lompe.*

lovløs saltlapskaus thick stew of salt pork, potatoes, and carrots, served with cranberry sauce and flatbread. See *lapskaus.*

lukket valnøtt marzipan-covered whipped-cream cake with a walnut and cream filling. TASTY

lutefisk dried fish, usually cod (*stokkfisk*), that has been lye-soaked in preparation for cooking. It has a jelly-like consistency after it has been soaked in lye. Pieces of boiled fish are topped with mustard sauce or melted butter and bits of bacon, and served with boiled potatoes and flatbread. *Lutefisk* is a traditional favorite at Christmastime. NATIONAL FAVORITE

lyr med løk pollack with onions.

lys lapskaus thick stew of meat, often salted, with root vegetables such as carrots, potatoes, rutabagas, and celeriac. See *lapskaus.* NATIONAL FAVORITE

løfbiff pancake-thin patty of ground beef, a popular fast food.

løksuppe onion soup.

løsebrød somewhat flattened, round rye buns with a deep notch dividing the buns into halves. They are a specialty of the coastal city of Bergen in Hordaland county in western Norway.

løyping curdled-milk soup made by adding buttermilk to boiling milk. It is typically served with bread.

makrellsuppe mackerel soup.

mandelbunn dessert with a base layer of ground almonds, whipped egg whites, and powdered sugar. Many different types of toppings are chosen to complete the dessert. DELICIOUS

mandelkaker almond cookies.

mandelpotetsuppe fra Grong creamy soup made with a variety of small almond-shaped potatoes, garnished with bacon and green onions. It is a specialty of Grong, a municipality of Nord-Trøndelag in central Norway.

marinert elgstek marinated moose roast.

marinert kveite marinated halibut.

marmorert fiskepudding layered fish pudding thickened with potato starch. Half the fish mixture is tinted pink. Alternating layers of tinted and untinted pudding are put in a loaf pan and baked. The pudding is served sliced. This dish comes from the county of Akershus in eastern Norway.

medisterkaker fried pork patties flavored with ginger. GOOD CHOICE

melboller flour dumplings.

NATIONAL FAVORITE **Mor Monsen** traditional sheet cake sprinkled with sugar, dried currants, and almonds. The cake is especially enjoyed at Christmastime. Whoever Mor Monsen (Mother Monsen) might have been has long been forgotten.

morrpølse fra Vegårdshei og Gjærstad fried cylinders of ground moose or beef spiced with ginger and allspice. This is a specialty of the neighboring municipalities of Vegårdshei and Gjærstad in southern Norway.

NATIONAL FAVORITE **multekrem** dessert made of cloudberries and whipped cream.

NATIONAL FAVORITE **multekrem i krumkaker** cloudberry cream served in *krumkake* cookie shells.

multer i gyllenbrun rømme cloudberries topped with a brown sugar and sour cream sauce.

multesuppe cloudberry dessert soup, served cold with cream.

REGIONAL CLASSIC **munkehatter fra Verdal** tart shells said to resemble monk hats, which are enjoyed with cloudberry cream (*multekrem*). This dessert comes from Verdal, a municipality in the county of Nord-Trøndelag in central Norway.

munker raised dough balls, similar to the Danish *aebleskiver*, flavored with cardamom. They are fried in a pan (*munkepanne*) that has small, round wells. See *eplemunker*.

myk krydderkake soft spice cake.

møsbrømlefse *lefse* spread with a melted brown-cheese mixture. This variation of *lefse* comes from the county of Nordland in northern Norway.

måneskinnspudding lemon-flavored, molded gelatin pudding with sweetened whipped cream and beaten egg whites, topped with beaten egg yolks and sugar.

Namdalsklenning oven-baked *lefse* made with barley and wheat flours, and brushed on the top with a mixture of cream and beaten eggs. After the *lefse* is baked, it is moistened with water, and the bottom side is spread with a mixture of butter, sugar, and cinnamon. Each circle is folded in half, buttered sides touching, and cut into wedges. The wedges are coated with a brown-cheese spread (*Namdalsgomme*) and rolled up like a crescent roll, starting with the wide edge. This intricate variation of *lefse* comes from Namdal, a traditional district in the county of Nord-Trøndelag in central Norway.

nedlagtsild marinated herring.

nepespa dish of dried lamb boiled with chopped rutabagas. The broth is lightly thickened with milk and flour and served as a side dish, along with soft flatbread (*lefse*). *Nepespa* is a traditional Christmas dish from Valle, a municipality in Aust-Agder county in southern Norway.

nøttekake med multebærfromasj nut cake with cloudberry mousse.   DELICIOUS

oksehalesuppe oxtail soup.

oksestek slices of roast beef in gravy.

ostekjeks med reddikkrem cheese crackers with radish cream.

overflodskake med bringebærfromasj cake with a base layer of   MUST HAVE
chopped hazelnuts and almonds, egg whites, and sugar, topped with raspberry mousse. The cake is garnished with an abundant assortment of fresh berries and fruit.

ovnsbakt kveite oven-baked halibut.

ovnsbakt steinbit med sjampinjongsaus og gulrotpuré oven-baked arctic catfish with mushroom sauce and carrot purée. See recipe, p. 66.

ovnsomelett oven-baked omelet.

ovnsstekt laks med honning og sennep roasted salmon with honey and mustard.

pakket nakke baked pork back and neck, served with a sweet-and-sour mixture of red cabbage, nuts, and raisins, and garnished with mushrooms in cream sauce.

pannebiff med salad pan-fried beefsteak with salad.

pannekaker large, crèpe-like pancakes made from batter without   NATIONAL FAVORITE
cultured milk or leavening agent. They are fried in a pan (*panne*) about 10 inches in diameter and are either folded in fourths or rolled up like a jelly roll when done. Sweet or savory foods may be incorporated into the batter or be spread on top after the pancake is fried. Compare with *lapper, sveler,* and *skjebladkadder.* These three pancake varieties are made from batter containing cultured milk and leavening agent, and are usually fried on a griddle or hot plate.

persetorsk cod fillets flattened under weight, then poached.

persille smør parsley butter.

persillebakt kveite på risotto av byggryn parsley-baked halibut served on barley risotto. See recipe, p. 51.

pinnefisk fish grilled on a stick.

pinnekjøtt lamb's ribs that are salted and dried, or sometimes smoked. They are traditionally steamed in a pot over small birch sticks (*pinne*) instead of in a metal steamer. This typical Christmas dish of western Norway is usually served with potatoes and mashed rutabagas.

platekake sheet cake sprinkled with cinnamon and sugar.

plommedessert plum dessert.

plukkfisk fish stew made from pieces of leftover fish "plucked" into small pieces.

Porsgrunnsdessert molded gelatin dessert made with eggs, gelatin, sugar, cream, shaved chocolate, rum, and raisins. It is a specialty of Porsgrunn, a town and a municipality in Telemark county in eastern Norway.

potetballer potato dumplings, usually made with grated raw potatoes held together with a little boiled potato. Other names for *potetballer* are *komler (kumler), raspeballer, baller, klubb,* or *klump,* depending on the region of the country.

potetgrøt potato porridge thickened with barley flour. It is a specialty of Telemark county in eastern Norway. Also called *jordeplegrøt.*

potetomelett potato omelet.

potetvafler potato waffles.

potteål boiled eel.

prinsefisk: dampet torskefilet på hvitvinsaus, med hummer og asparges "fish for a prince": steamed cod fillets in white wine sauce, with lobster and asparagus. It is a specialty of the city of Bergen in Hordaland county in western Norway. See recipe, p. 55.

pytt i panne hash, often served topped with a fried egg.

pærer fra Hardanger dessert of pear halves cooked in water with lingonberry jam, sugar, and cinnamon. It is served with crispy waffle cookies (*krumkaker*) and whipped cream. Hardanger, a traditional district in Hordaland county in western Norway, surrounds Hardangerfjord and is Norway's orchard.

pølse i lompe hot dog eaten in a potato pancake. It is a popular street food.

pølsesuppe med byggryn sausage soup with barley.

rabarbradrikk drink made with fresh rhubarb. See recipe, p. 45.

rabarbrafromasj mousse of sweetened, cooked rhubarb in whipped gelatin and fresh orange juice.

rabarbragrøt rhubarb fool. See recipe, p. 70. GOOD CHOICE

rabarbrakake rhubarb cake.

rabarbrasuppe rhubarb soup.

rakørret kokt i øl fermented trout poached in beer.

raspeballer potato dumplings. See *potetballer*. NATIONAL FAVORITE

raspeballer med kjøtt og kålrabistappe grated potato dumplings with meat and mashed rutabagas.

reinsdyrfilet fylt med geitost fillet of reindeer stuffed with brown cheese (*geitost*) from goat's milk whey. See recipe, p. 62.

reinsdyrfilet med fløtesaus fillet of reindeer with cream sauce. See recipe, p. 69.

reinsdyrfilet på purre og soppseng fillet of reindeer on a bed of creamed leeks and mushrooms.

reinsdyrstek med rødvinsaus reindeer roast with red wine sauce.

reinstek reindeer roast.

rekeboller shrimp balls.

reker med majones shrimp with mayonnaise. DELICIOUS

rekesalat shrimp salad.

ribberulle thinly sliced cold cuts made from a brined and boiled NATIONAL FAVORITE
meat roll—typically lamb or beef flank steak—which is flattened, topped with fatty pork and spices, rolled up, and tied. After the *ribberulle* has been boiled, it is weighted down to form a rectangular shape and chilled. *Ribberulle,* a traditional Christmas offering, is often called by its Danish name, *rullepølse.*

ribbestek med rødkål rib roast with red cabbage.

rike riddere "rich knights," a baked dessert of bread soaked in a mixture of milk, eggs, and sugar, then sprinkled with cinnamon and sliced almonds. It is topped with jam and whipped cream or vanilla ice cream. Compare with a simpler version of this dessert, *arme riddere,* or "poor knights."

rips med vaniljesaus currants with vanilla sauce.

ris lapp small, thick pancake made with rice.

ris med tyttebær dessert of rice with lingonberries.

ris og sviskedessert rice and prune dessert.

risengrynsgrøt creamed rice or rice porridge.

riskrem rice cream, an almond-flavored dessert made with rice, NATIONAL FAVORITE
milk, sugar, and whipped cream. It usually is served with a slightly thickened fruit sauce. *Riskrem* traditionally is a dessert eaten on Christmas Eve. A whole almond is added to pudding

made at this time and the person who finds the nut is given a special present.

REGIONAL CLASSIC **Rogalandskringle** glazed cardamom-flavored coffee cake in the shape of a figure eight, with raisins and candied lemon peel. It is a specialty of Rogaland county in western Norway.

rognkaker fried cakes made of roe mixed with mashed potatoes, egg, and milk.

NATIONAL FAVORITE **rosettbakkelser** rosettes, crispy deep-fried cookies made with a special rosette iron (*rosettbakkelsjern*). The *rosettbakkelser* are sprinkled with powdered sugar or topped with whipped cream and jam. They are a traditional Christmas favorite.

rosmarinkrydrete lammekoteletter lamb cutlets seasoned with rosemary. It is a specialty of Troms, a county in northern Norway.

NATIONAL FAVORITE **rullepølse** thinly sliced cold cuts made from a brined and boiled meat roll. See *ribberulle*.

rypa i gryta mountain ptarmigan cooked with milk and brown goat cheese (*geitost*), and served with brown sauce flavored with juniper. This dish comes from the municipality of Voss in Hordaland county in western Norway.

rødgrøt med fløtemelk porridge made with cream, raspberry or black-currant juice, cinnamon, sugar, cloves, and potato starch.

rømmefromasj sour-cream mousse.

NATIONAL FAVORITE **rømmegrøt** sour-cream porridge. See recipe, p. 49.

REGIONAL CLASSIC **rømmegrøt fra Sogn og Fjordane** sour-cream porridge topped with raisins, sugar, cinnamon, and chopped, hard-boiled egg. This variation of *rømmegrøt* is from Sogn og Fjordane, a county in western Norway.

DELICIOUS **rømmestekt fjellørret** fried mountain trout with sour-cream sauce.

røykt laks og eggerøre smoked salmon with scrambled eggs.

røykt ål smoked eel.

rådyrmedaljonger med rips roe deer medallions with currants.

rådyrpostei med enerbær og akevitt roe deer terrine with juniper and aquavit.

rådyrsadel med glaserte gulerøtter saddle of roe deer with glazed carrots.

råmelkspudding raw-milk pudding.

safranbrød saffron buns.

salt fleskekjøtt og pølse med ertesuppe salt pork and sausage with yellow pea soup.

saltfiskballer fra Frøya boiled, salted fish balls with pieces of brown goat cheese (*geitost*) in the center. The fish balls are made of fish, raw and cooked potatoes, cream, and corn syrup. Boiled potatoes, mashed rutabagas, and pieces of salt pork accompany the dish, which is a speciality of the island of Frøya in Sør-Trøndelag county in central Norway.

saltkjøttsuppe og kålstappe soup with salted meat and mashed rutabagas. Regional variations include beef, lamb, or pork, or a combination of the three.

Sandefjordsmør classic fish sauce with butter, cream, and parsley or chives, which was inspired by the French sauce *beurre blanc*. It is named for Sandefjord, a city and municipality in Vestfold county in eastern Norway.

sandkaker rich, buttery Christmas cookies made with ground almonds. The dough is pressed into special molds and baked.

sandterte cake made with butter, sugar, eggs, and flour, but without a leavening agent.

sardinpålegg sardine spread.

saupskringle fra Telemark pretzel-shaped, cardamom-flavored coffee cake, made with buttermilk, sour cream, and raisins. It is from Telemark, a county in eastern Norway.

seibiff med løk fried saithe steaks and onions. Saithe is a type of cod.

seikaker ground saithe cakes. Saithe is a type of cod.

selskapskrokanpudding festive molded gelatin dessert topped with crumbled almond brittle. It comes from Hedmark, a county in eastern Norway.

semuleboller til søt suppe semolina dumplings with raisins, chopped almonds, and lemon zest. These dumplings are enjoyed in sweet soups.

semulepudding milk pudding made with semolina.

sherrysild salted herring in sherry.

sild i sennepssaus herring in mustard sauce.

sildegrynssuppe soup with salted herring, barley, and vegetables.

silpo salt pork and potatoes, stewed in milk. This dish comes from Finnskogen, an area in the traditional district of Solør, in Hedmark county in eastern Norway.

sirupssnipper diamond-shaped cookies with a blanched almond in the center. They are a traditional Christmas cookie.

sjokolade og myntekake mint chocolate cake. See recipe, p. 74.

sjokolade roll chocolate roll (jelly roll).

sjokoladepudding med vaniljesaus chocolate pudding with vanilla sauce.

sjokoladeris sweet dessert made with rice, chocolate, and egg yolk.

skalldyrsalat shellfish salad.

skillingsboller yeast-raised cinnamon rolls. This treat comes from the city of Bergen in Hordaland county in western Norway.

GOOD CHOICE **skinkebiff** ham steak.

skinkeomelett ham omelet.

skjebladkaker Tiny, cultured-milk pancakes with leavening agent made with the amount of batter that can fill the bowl of a spoon (*skjeblad*). See *lapper* and *pannekaker*.

skranglekål dish of boiled lamb or pork shank, oatmeal, and milk.

smalaføtter lamb's feet.

REGIONAL CLASSIC **smalahove** salted, smoked, and boiled half of a lamb's head, without brains, served with mashed rutabagas and a whole, unpeeled, boiled potato. It is a traditional dish of western Norway, especially the municipality of Voss in Hordaland county, and is enjoyed in the fall and at Christmas.

smultringer doughnuts fried in lard.

REGIONAL CLASSIC **småmat** clear soup with finely diced pieces of meat, vegetables, and potatoes. It comes from Hallingdal, a traditional district in Buskerud county in eastern Norway.

smått og godt fra Sandefjord dessert of strawberries, cherry liqueur, sugar, cream, and slivered almonds. It is a treat from Sandefjord, a town and municipality in Vestfold county in eastern Norway.

Snåsaklubb med flesk og duppe dumplings made from barley flour and potatoes. Some syrup and a piece of brown cheese is tucked inside the dumplings. They are served with salt pork and brown cheese sauce. *Snåsaklubb* is a specialty of Snåsa, a municipality in the county of Nord-Trøndelag in central Norway.

sommerlig kveite fra Kjeurda i Jøsenfjorden summer halibut from Kjeurda in Jøsen Fjord. See recipe, p. 63.

Sondagslefse fra Rogaland Sunday griddle-fried "Sunday" *lefse* made with dough containing buttermilk and syrup. After the *lefse* is fried, it is spread with a sweetened mixture of egg, butter, and chocolate, folded in half, and cut into wedges. It is a specialty of Rogaland county in western Norway.

sonning fra Vinje i Telemark stew of several salted meats with barley, peas, turnips, and potatoes. It is served with onion sauce. The dish comes from Vinje, a municipality in Telemark county in eastern Norway.

soppsuppe mushroom soup.

sosekjøtt hearty soup with chunks of beef.

speilegg fried egg.

spekemat med eggerøre cured meat with scrambled eggs.

spekesild med gulrøtter marinated salted herring with carrots.

spekesild med løk og tomat marinated salted herring with onions   GOOD CHOICE
and tomatoes.

spekesild med rømmesaus marinated salted herring with sour-
cream sauce.

sprø kanelkake crisp cake with several thin, cinnamon-flavored
layers separated by whipped cream. The top layer is spread with
chocolate.

sprøstekt lyr med saltbakte røbeter crispy pollack served with
salt-baked beets. See recipe, p. 68.

sprøstekt sild crispy, fried fresh herring.

sprøstekte torsketunger crispy, fried cod "tongues," which
actually come from a triangular muscle in the floor of the mouth.

Stavangersild salted herring topped with an egg, mustard sauce,   REGIONAL CLASSIC
and vinegar sauce. This dish comes from the coastal city of
Stavanger in Rogaland county in western Norway.

steinbitfilet med løk og kaperser fillet of arctic catfish with onions   DELICIOUS
and capers.

steinkjerkaker cinnamon- and almond-flavored sugar cookies.
They are a specialty of Nord-Trøndelag county in central
Norway.

stekt and roasted duck.

stekt flesk og duppe fried slices of salt pork. A sauce (*duppe*),
made by whisking milk into the hot pork drippings, is ladled
over sliced boiled potatoes. Root vegetables typically are served
with this specialty of Telemark county in eastern Norway.

stekt kylling med kålrotstuing braised chicken with mashed
rutabagas.

stekt laks med fløtesaus fried salmon with cream sauce.

stekt lever med bacon og løk fried liver with bacon and onions.

stekt tørrfisk fried rehydrated dried cod.

Stiftsgårdskaken cobbler-like cake made with apples and almonds.
It is a dish from Stiftsgården, the King's residence in Trondheim
in Sør-Trøndelag county in central Norway.

stuet tørrfisk creamed rehydrated dried cod.

stuete erter creamed peas.

stuete (stuede) jordskokker med forlorent egg creamed Jerusalem
artichokes topped with a poached egg.

sukkervafler sugar waffles.

EXCELLENT **supansuppe** soup with potatoes and three meats—smoked lamb, pork sausages, and slab bacon—cut into small dice. The broth is thickened with a little flour and buttermilk. Crisp flatbread is crumbled on top of the soup.

surbrød round, flat sour bread with crushed caraway seeds. Traditionally, holes were made in the center of the bread so the loaves could be hung on rods near the ceiling to dry. *Surbrød* is from Finnmark county in northern Norway.

NATIONAL FAVORITE **surkål** sauerkraut—cabbage cooked with vinegar, sugar, and caraway. It is a traditional dish for Christmas dinner.

REGIONAL CLASSIC **sveler** griddle-fried, cultured-milk pancakes with leavening agent, spread with butter and sugar, jam, or cheese, and folded in half. A specialty of the traditional district of Sunnmøre in Møre og Romsdal county in western Norway, *sveler* are popular fast food on the ferries in the Sunnmøre fjords. See *lapper* and *skjebladkaker*. Also see *pannekaker,* crêpe-like pancakes without cultured milk or leavening agents in the batter.

svineribbe pork rib roast.

svinestek med frukt roast pork loin with fruit.

svinestek med rødkål roast pork loin with red cabbage.

sylte head cheese. Meat from a pig's head is layered with spices and poached. The meat is pressed and usually brined before slicing. *Sylte* is a traditional sandwich filling at Christmastime.

syltet makrell pickled mackerel.

syltete rødbeter pickled beetroot.

syltelabber boiled, salted pig's trotters, which usually are eaten around Christmastime.

REGIONAL CLASSIC **Sørlandets solskinnsdessert** peaches and plums cooked in sugar syrup and topped with cream sauce. This dessert comes from southern Norway.

tang- og skalldyrsuppe fra Tromsø creamy soup with kelp and shellfish. It comes from Tromsø, a city and municipality in Troms county in northern Norway.

Telemarksknuter dessert of baked apples enclosed in pastry. The apple is placed in the middle of a pastry square and the four corners of the pastry are brought up over the center of the apple and pinched together, giving the dessert the appearance of a knot. This dessert is a specialty of Telemark county in eastern Norway.

NATIONAL FAVORITE **tilslørte bondepiker** "veiled peasant girls," a layered dessert of caramelized bread crumbs, stewed apples, and whipped cream.

It is said that the name of this dessert implies that a fancy dish has been concocted from ordinary ingredients. The top layer of cream is the "veil."

timianristet laks salmon fried in thyme.

torskefilet med urtesmør cod fillet with herbed butter. **GOOD CHOICE**

torskehoder cod heads.

torskesuppe cod soup.

torsketunger på bergensk manér Bergen-style cod "tongues" dipped in beaten eggs, rolled in breadcrumbs, and fried. Bergen is a coastal city in Hordaland county in western Norway.

tradisjonell viltsaus traditional game sauce with sour cream, brown goat cheese (*geitost*), and juniper berries.

trollkrem troll cream, a dessert of beaten egg whites and sugar **NATIONAL FAVORITE** mixed with berries, usually lingonberries. It is a common fall and winter dish.

Trondhjemssuppe thick, sweet-and-sour milk soup made with with rice, raisins, currant or raspberry juice, sugar, and cream or sour cream. The soup is served hot. It comes from Trondheim, a city and municipality in Sør-Trøndelag county in central Norway.

tyttingkir drink of lingonberry juice, white wine, and sugar.

tyttebærgrøt med fløte lingonberry porridge with cream.

tørrfisk i tomatsaus rehydrated dried fish cooked in tomato sauce.

tårn-tærte "tower tart" constructed from a stack of almond wafer **REGIONAL CLASSIC** cookies of increasingly smaller diameter and held together with layers of thick jam. The finished tart is glazed with powdered sugar. This treat comes from Akershus county in eastern Norway.

urteloff herb bread.

urtemarinert reinsdyrstek med rømmesaus herb-marinated roast of reindeer with sour-cream sauce.

urtestekt medaljonger av breiflabb herb-fried medallions of anglerfish.

vafler med syltetøy waffles with jam. **NATIONAL FAVORITE**

vaktel i fløtesaus quail in cream sauce.

vaniljehjerter heart-shaped vanilla Christmas cookies.

NATIONAL FAVORITE   **verdens beste** "world's best" cake. Both of the rich, buttery cake layers are topped with meringue and almonds before they are baked. Also called *kvæfjordkake*.

Vesterålens blåbærsuppe med fløteisterninger blueberry soup served with a cube of frozen whipped cream. It comes from Vesterålens, which comprises six municipalities in Nordland county in northern Norway.

REGIONAL CLASSIC   **viltgryte med finnbiff og sjampinjong** stew of shaved reindeer meat (*finnbiff*), mushrooms, and bacon in a sour cream and brown goat cheese (*geitost*) sauce, flavored with juniper berries. The dish is also called simply *finnbiff*. See *finnbiff*.

vinkandel fra Grimstad dessert soup made from boiled wine and water, flavored with cinnamon and lemon peel, and thickened with egg yolks beaten with sugar. It is served with whipped cream. The soup is attributed to Grimstad, a town and municipality in Aust-Agder county in southern Norway.

Vossabia honningbrød honey bread made from Vossabia honey, a product from the Vossabia (the Voss Bee) apiary in the municipality of Voss in western Norway. See recipe, p. 72.

vørterkake "malt cake" made with non-alcoholic malt beer (*vørterøl*). It is a traditional Christmas cake from Vest-Agder county in southern Norway.

wienerbrød Danish pastry. It is very popular in Norway.

Foods & Flavors Guide

This chapter is a comprehensive list of foods, spices, kitchen utensils, and cooking terminology in Norwegian, with English translations. We have omitted most Norwegian words that are close to or the same as those in English. The list will be helpful in interpreting menus and for shopping in Norway's markets. As a rule, market vendors identify their products by name and by price (in *krone,* NOK), which is determined by weight or by the piece. If an item is not identified, however, it is useful to know how to say, "What is this called?" See *Helpful Phrases,* p. 79.

abbor European perch (*Perca fluviatilis*).
aftens light meal before bed. Also called *aftensmat.*
agurk cucumber; gherkin; pickle.
akevitt national drink of Norway, distilled from potatoes. It is flavored with caraway and/or dill. Also spelled *aquavit.*
akkar squid; also called *blekksprutt,* as is octopus.
alkoholfri drikk non-alcoholic beverage.
allehånde allspice.
alminnelig brød light rye bread.
alperips mountain currant (*Ribes alpinum*), a small, juicy berry resembling a red currant.
ananas pineapple.
and duck.
anis aniseed; also called *anisfrø.*
ansjos anchovy.
appelsin orange.
appelsinjuice orange juice.
appelsinmarmelade orange marmalade.
appetittvekker appetizer.
aprikos apricot.
aquavit national drink of Norway distilled from potatoes. Also spelled *akevitt.*

FOODS & FLAVORS GUIDE

artisjokk artichoke.

artisjokkbunn artichoke heart.

asparges asparagus.

avkokt boiled or poached. Also called simply *kokt*. Another word for poached is *posjert*.

bakepulver baking powder.

bakstehelle large griddle for cooking *flatbrød* and *lefse*.

bakverk pastry.

barnemeny children's menu.

basilikum basil.

bekkørret brook trout or char (*Salvelinus fontinalis*); also called *bekkerøye*.

benløs boned.

bergmynte oregano.

bete beet.

biff beefsteak.

biffkam sirloin.

bindsalat romaine lettuce or cos lettuce; also called *romanosalat* and *romersalat*.

bjørnebær blackberry or brambleberry (*Rubus fructicosus*). The fruit is eaten fresh or made into jams and desserts.

bladbete Swiss chard; also called *mangold*.

bladsalat leaf lettuce.

bladselleri celery.

blek piggsopp hedgehog mushroom (*Hydnum repandum*), a delicious, irregular-shaped fungus with a centrally depressed cap and a slightly off-center stem. The mushroom gets its name from the resemblance of the small, tooth-like spines on the underside of the cap to a hedgehog. Also called simply *piggsopp*.

blekksprut octopus or squid. Another word for squid is *akkar*.

blod blood.

blodig rare; underdone (as meat, for example). Another word for *blodig* is *råstekt*.

blokkebær bog bilberry (*Vaccinium uliginosum*); also called bog whortleberry. The sweet, blue-black berries have white flesh.

blomkål cauliflower.

blåbringebær European dewberry (*Rubus caesius*), purple to black berries resembling raspberries. The fruit is eaten fresh or made into jams and pies.

blåbær blueberry (*Vaccinium corymbosum*); also the name for closely related berries such as the bilberry (*Vaccinium myrtillus*), a blue-black berry

112

resembling the blueberry, but smaller, with red or purple fruit pulp. The fruit is eaten fresh or made into jams, juices, and pies.

blåkrabbe blue crab (*Callinectes sapidus*).

blåkveite Greenland halibut or blue halibut (*Reinhardtius hippoglossoides*).

blåmuggost blue cheese.

blåskjell mussel or blue mussel (*Mytilus edulis*).

bokhvete buckwheat.

bokkøl strong, dark beer.

boknafisk partially dried fish, often cod. The fish is gutted and hung in the sun and wind until the exterior is dry and the interior is still moist and slightly sour. Also the name of the dish made with partially dried fish; see *Menu Guide*.

bokstavhummer Norway lobster (*Nephrops norvegicus*), a slim, orange-colored lobster in the northeastern Atlantic. Also called *sjøkreps*.

bolle fish or meatball; also the name for a dumpling or a bun.

bondebønne broad bean or fava bean (*Vicia faba*); also called *fevesbønne* and *hestebønne*.

bondemåten country style.

bord table.

bordduk table cloth.

bordvin table wine.

boysenbær boysenberry (*Rubus ursinus* × *idaeus*).

brasme fresh water bream (*Abramis brama*).

brasmeflire blue bream (*Abramis ballerus*).

bredbladet endivie escarole or broad-leaved endive (*Cichorium endivia* var. *latifolia*). Also called *eskariolsalat*.

breiflabb anglerfish; monkfish (*Lophius piscatorius*).

brekkbønne green bean.

brennevin spirits; liquor.

bresert braised.

bringebær raspberry (*Rubis ideaus*).

brisling European sprat (*Sprattus sprattus*).

brissel sweetbreads.

brokkoli broccoli.

brosme cusk; tusk (*Brosme brosme*), a cod-like marine fish.

brun bønne kidney bean; brown bean.

brun saus gravy served with most meats, meatcakes, sausages, and fishcakes.

brunost general term for brown cheese made from whey, the watery portion of milk that remains after whole milk is curdled to make "white" cheese.

Traditionally, *brunost* is made with goat's-milk whey and is called *geitost*. Strictly speaking, if the whey contains no additives, the cheese is called *mysost*. If the cheese is made from cow's-milk whey it is called *fløtemysost*.

brunt sucker brown sugar.

brus soda pop; also called *leskedrikk*.

bryggeri brewery.

bryst breast.

brød bread.

brødkorn grain; cereal. Also called simply *korn*.

brødskive slice of bread.

brødsmuler bread crumbs.

brønnkarse watercress.

bukkehornkløver fenugreek.

buljong bouillon.

butterdeig puff pastry; also called *smørdeig*.

bygg barley.

byggmel barley flour.

byggryn pearl barley.

bær berry.

bøkling smoked herring.

bønne bean.

bønnespirer bean sprouts.

daddel date.

dagens suppe soup of the day.

dagligvareforretning grocery store.

dampet steamed.

deig dough.

desserter desserts or sweet dishes.

dillfrø dill seed.

drikke drink.

drikkepenger tip; gratuity.

drikkepenger inkludert tip included.

drikkevann drinking water.

drikkevarer drinks; beverages.

drue grape.

druebrennevin brandy.

duppe sauce made from pork drippings.

durra sorghum.

durumhvete durum wheat.

durumhvetemel durum wheat flour.

dypvannsreke deep-water shrimp.

dyr general term for animal; also means deer. Another word for deer is *hjort*. Deer in Norway usually refers to the widespread species known as red deer (*Cervus elaphus*). *Rådyr*, or roe deer (*Capreolus capreolus*), is also common in Norway. *Reinsdyr* (*Rangifer tarandus*) is reindeer.

dyrekjøtt deer meat; venison. Also called *hjortekjøtt*.

dyrestek venison roast.

eddik vinegar.

edelkreps crayfish or crawfish; also called *ferskvannskreps*, or simply *kreps*.

edelplomme greengage (*Prunus domestica insititia*), a yellow-green fruit related to the plum.

eggehvite egg white.

eggekrem egg custard.

eggeplomme egg yolk.

eggfrukt eggplant.

eikebladsalat oakleaf lettuce (*Lactuca sativa crispa*), a type of loose-leaf lettuce. Available in red and green varieties.

einebær juniper berry.

elg moose; European elk (*Alces alces*).

endivie curly endive or chicory (*Cichorium endivia* var. *crispum*). Also called *endivsalat* and *krusendivie*.

eple apple.

epleeddik cider vinegar.

ert pea.

eskariolsalat escarole or broad-leaved endive (*Cichorium endivia* var. *latifolia*). Also called *bredbladet endivie*.

estragon tarragon.

ettermiddagste afternoon tea.

farin granulated sugar.

farse filling or stuffing.

fatøl draft beer.

fennikel fennel.

ferdigmat fast food.

fersk fresh.

fersken peach.

ferskost fresh cheese.

ferskvannsfisk freshwater fish.

ferskvannskreps freshwater crayfish; also called *edelkreps* or simply *kreps*.

fett fat or lard.

fevesbønne broad bean or fava bean (*Vicia faba*); also called *bondebønne* and *hestebønne*.

fiken fig.

filodeig phyllo pastry dough.

finbrød rye bread.

finhakket finely chopped.

finnbiff shaved frozen reindeer meat. Literally means "Finnish steak." Also called *reinsdyrskav*.

firetrådet fourbeard rockling (*Enchelyopus cimbrius*), a fish in the cod family. Also called *tangbrosme*.

fisk fish.

fiskeretter fish dishes, a term seen as a header on menus.

fjellkrekling mountain crowberry (*Empetrum nigrum* subsp. *hermaphroditum*), a sweet, bluish-black fruit that resembles and tastes like a blueberry. The berries grow on a low evergreen shrub and are used to make juice and jams. Also called simply *krekling*.

fjellrype rock or mountain ptarmigan (*Lagopus muta*), a game bird in the grouse family. Also called simply *rype*.

fjellørret mountain lake trout.

fjærkre poultry; also spelled *fjørfe*.

flaskeøl bottled beer.

flatbrød flatbread or crispbread.

flesk fatty pork such as pork belly, which is typically salted and cured, but usually not smoked. It often is ground or sliced. Pork meat in general is called *gris, grisekjøtt,* or *svinekjøtt.*

flire white sea bream (*Diplodus sargus*).

flormelis powdered sugar.

flyndre European flounder (*Platichthys flesus*).

fløte cream.

fløtekaramell toffee.

fløtemysost whey cheese made from cow's milk. See *brunost.*

forlorent egg poached egg.

formkake loaf cake.

forrett appetizer.

franskbrød white bread.

frikassé stew.

fritert deep-fried.

frokost breakfast.

fromasj mousse.

froskelår frog's legs.

frukt fruit.

fruktgelé fruit jelly.

frø kernel or seed. Also called *kjerne.*

fullkornbrød whole-wheat bread. Also called *helkornbrød.*

furumatriske saffron milk-cap (*Lactarius deliciosus*), a bright-orange mushroom that oozes drops of orange "milk."

får lamb or mutton. Another word for lamb or mutton is *sau.* Both words refer to the animal (*sau* more so) as well as the meat. Specific words for the meat are *fårekjøtt* and *sauekjøtt.*

fårekjøtt lamb (meat) or mutton. Also called *sauekjøtt.* Also see *får* and *sau.*

gaffel fork.

gammelost pungent, brownish-yellow, granular cheese made from skim milk that is allowed to sour prior to heating it. The curds that result are pressed into forms, and when the cheese is removed from them it is inoculated with a mold, typically *Penicillium roqueforti.* This produces greenish-blue veining and the characteristic strong flavor and aroma of the cheese.

gauda gouda cheese.

geit goat.

geitmelk goat milk.

geitost whey cheese made with goat's milk. See *brunost.*

gelé jelly. Refers to both gelatin desserts and aspic.

gjedde northern pike (*Esox lucius*).

gjær yeast.

gjørs pike-perch (*Sander spp.*), a genus of fish in the perch family that resembles the unrelated pike.

glasert glazed.

glasur icing; frosting.

gotteri candy. Also called is *sukkertøy.*

granateple pomegranate.

gravet marinated.

gresskar squash; pumpkin.

gresskarmarmelade pumpkin marmalade.

gressløk chive.

grille grill; broil.

gris pig or pork. Another word for pig is *svin*. Pork is also called *grisekjøtt* and *svinekjøtt*.

grisekjøtt pork. See *gris*.

grovbrød coarse, dark bread such as rye or pumpernickel.

gryn groats, hulled grains of cereals.

grytestekt braised; also see *stekt*.

grønn green; fresh.

grønn bønne green bean.

grønn pepper green pepper.

grønnkål kale.

grønnmynte spearmint.

grønnsak vegetable.

grønnsaker og sopper vegetables and mushrooms.

grønnsakshandel vegetable market.

grønnsaksjuice vegetable juice.

grøt porridge.

grågås graylag, a wild goose.

gul ert yellow pea.

gulrot carrot.

gurkemeie turmeric.

gås goose.

haneskjell Iceland scallop (*Chlamys islandica*), a prized variety commonly found north of Trøndelag.

hardkokt hard-boiled.

harr grayling (*Thymallus thymallus*), a fish in the salmon family. Harr has a slight scent of thyme, which accounts for its scientific name.

hasselnøtt hazelnut.

hasselnøttolje hazelnut oil.

havabbor sea bass (*Dicentrarchus labrax,* or *Morone labrax*).

havkaruss black sea bream (*Spondyliosoma cantharus*).

havre oats.

havregryn rolled oats; oat groats.

havremel oat flour.

helfet ost full-fat cheese.

helkornbrød whole-wheat bread. Also called *fullkornbrød*.

helmelk whole milk. Sometimes it is written *h-melk*.

helstekt roasted; also see *stekt*.

hermetikk canned goods; preserves.

hestebønne broad bean or fava bean (*Vicia faba*). Also called *bondebønne* and *fevesbønne*.

hestekjøtt horse meat.

hetvin fortified wine. Also called *sterkvin*.

hirse millet.

hjemmelaget homemade.

hjerne brain.

hjerte heart.

hjort deer; see *dyr*.

hjortekjøtt venison. Also called *dyrekjøtt*.

hjortetakk hartshorn salt (hornsalt), or baker's ammonia (ammonium carbonate), orginally ground from deer's (hart's) antlers, and used as a leavening agent. Since ammonia gas is given off during baking, it is important to work in a well-ventilated room. An equivalent amount of baking powder can be substituted for *hjortetakk*.

hodekål white head cabbage (*Brassica oleracea* var. *alba*). Also called *hvitkål*.

hodesalat head lettuce; cabbage lettuce.

honning honey.

honningmelon honeydew melon.

hovedrett main dish.

hummer lobster (*Homarus gammarus*).

husets "house" specialty.

husmannskost traditional food.

hval whale.

hvete wheat.

hvetebrød wheat bread.

hvetekim wheat germ.

hvetemel wheat flour.

hvit white.

hvit asparges white asparagus.

hvit bønne white bean; navy bean.

hvit løk white onion.

hvit pepper white pepper.

hvit sjokolade white chocolate.

hvite egg white.

hvitkål white cabbage. Another word for white cabbage is *hodekål.*

hvitløk garlic.

hvitsaus white sauce or gravy.

hvitting whiting (*Merlangus merlangus*), a fish in the cod family. It is named for its white, flaky flesh.

hvitvin white wine.

hyllebær elderberry.

hyse haddock (*Melanogrammus aeglefinus*). Also called *kolje.*

høne hen; chicken. Refers to the animal, not the meat, which is *kylling.*

hønsebuljong chicken bouillon.

høyrygg chuck (cut of beef).

indrefilet tenderloin.

ingefær ginger.

innmat offal; variety meats.

is ice; also means sherbet and ice cream. Another word for ice cream is *iskrem.*

ishavsrøye arctic char (*Salvelinus alpinus*), a freshwater and saltwater fish that is closely related to the trout and the salmon. Also called *røye* and *sjørøye.*

issalat iceberg lettuce.

iste iced tea.

isvann ice water.

jerpe hazel hen or hazel grouse (*Tetrastes bonasia*).

jordbær strawberry.

jordnøtt peanut; also called *peanøtt.*

jordnøttolje peanut oil.

jordskokk Jerusalem artichoke.

kaffe med fløte coffee with cream.

kajennepepper cayenne pepper.

kakao cocoa.

kake cake or cookie. Other names for cookie are *kjeks* and *småkake*.

kald cold.

kalkun turkey.

kalmar calamari.

kalvebrissel veal sweetbreads. The general term for sweetbreads is *brissel*.

kalvefilet filet of veal.

kalvekjøtt veal.

kalvelever calf's liver.

kamillete chamomile tea.

kammusling scallop meat.

kamskjell literally scallop shell; also can mean scallop meat. It is the name of the king scallop, great scallop, or Saint-Jacques scallop (*Pecten maximus*). Also called *stort kamskjell*.

kandisert candied.

kanel cinnamon.

kanin rabbit.

kantarell common chanterelle mushroom (*Cantharellus cibarius*).

karbonade meat patty made with lean ground meat (*karbonadedeig*). Both the cooked and uncooked meat patty are called *karbonade*. Also called *karbonadekake*.

karbonadedeig lean ground meat that has a maximum of 6 percent fat. It is used to make patties (*karbonader*; singular *karbonade*). Compare with the fattier ground meat product, *kjøttdeig*.

kardemomme cardamom.

karse garden cress; also called *matkarse*.

kart unripe fruit or berry.

karve caraway; also called *spisskarve*.

kasjunøtt cashew nut.

kasserollesteke pot roast.

kastanje chestnut.

kepaløk yellow onion.

kikert chickpea or garbanzo bean.

kirsebær cherry.

kje kid, or young goat.

kjeks cracker or cookie; also see *kake* and *småkake*.

kjerne kernel or seed; also called *frø*.

kjernemelk buttermilk.

kjevle rolling pin.

kjøkkensjef executive chef.

kjørvel chervil.

kjøtt meat.

kjøttbolle meatball; also called *kjøttkake.*

kjøttbuljong meat bouillon.

kjøttdeig ground meat. This meat product can contain up to 14 percent fat. It typically is used in casseroles and fast foods like pizza, in which ground meat is not the primary component of the dish. Compare with the leaner ground meat product, *karbonadedeig.*

kjøttmat meat or food containing meat.

kjøttretter meat dishes, a term seen as a header on menus.

kli bran.

klippfisk "cliff fish," salted and dried fish, especially cod, which traditionally were placed on rocky cliffs near the shore during the summer to dry in the sun and wind. Also see *stokkfisk* and *tørrfisk.*

knekkebrød crispbread; rye crispbread.

knivskjell European razor clam (*Solen vagina*).

knutekål kohlrabi (*Brassica oleracea* var. *gongylodes*). The vegetable known in Norway as *kålrabi* (also *kålrot*) is the rutabaga, not the kohlrabi.

kokebanan plantain.

kokosnøtt coconut.

kokt boiled; poached. Also called *avkokt.* Another word for poached is *posjert.*

kokt egg hard-boiled egg.

koldtbord "cold table," a buffet of cold dishes. It is more commonly known in the United States by the Swedish word *smørgåsbord.*

kolje haddock (*Melanogrammus aeglefinus*). Also called *hyse.*

konditori pastry shop.

konditorvare pastry.

kongekrabbe red king crab (*Paralithodes camtschatica*).

kopp cup.

korint fresh or dried currant.

korketrekker corkscrew.

korn grain; cereals. Also called *brødkorn.*

kornfrokost breakfast cereal.

korv Swedish word for sausage that is used in some areas of Norway. The Norwegian word for sausage is *pølse.* Also spelled *kurv.*

kost food; another word for food is *mat.*

kotelett cutlet; chop.

kotelettkam rib.

kraft soup stock.

krekling mountain crowberry (*Empetrum nigrum* subsp. *hermaphroditum*). Also called *fjellkrekling*.

krem whipped cream; also called *pisket krem*.

kremfløte whipping cream.

kremle a mushroom of the *Russula* genus, several of which are edible and prized. For example, see *mandelkremle*.

kremortartari cream of tartar.

kremost cream cheese.

kremsuppe cream soup.

kreps freshwater crayfish. Also called *edelkreps* and *ferskvannskreps*.

kronhjort red deer (*Cervus elaphus*).

krusemynte garden mint.

krusendivie curly chicory or endive (*Cichorium endivia* var. *crispum*); also called *endivie* and *endivsalat*.

kruspersille parsley; also called simply *persille*.

krydder spices; seasonings.

kryddereddik spicy vinegar.

krypberglyng wintergreen or teaberry. Also called *vintergrønn*.

krøkle smelt.

kråkebolle sea urchin (*Echinus esculentus*).

krås giblets; gizzard.

ku cow.

kullsyret carbonated.

kumle potato dumpling; also called *potetball* and *raspeball*.

kurv sausage, in Swedish. See *korv*.

kvede quince.

kveite Atlantic halibut (*Hippoglossus hippoglossus*).

kveldsmat evening meal.

kvern food grinder; mill.

kylling chicken; also see *høne*.

kål cabbage.

kålrabi rutabaga or swede (*Brassica napus* var. *napobrassica*). Other names for rutabaga are *kålrot* and *sukkernepe*. Note that the kohlrabi (*Brassica oleracea* var. *gongylodes*) is not called *kålrabi* but *knutekål* in Norwegian.

lagesild vendace (*Coregonus albulathe*), the European whitefish.

lake burbot (*Lota lota*), a cod-like freshwater fish.

laks salmon (*Salmo salar*).

laksabbor black bass or largemouth black bass (*Micropterus salmoides*). Also called *ørretabbor*.

lam lamb.

lammekjøtt lamb (meat); mutton.

landvin local wine.

lange ling (*Molva molva*), a large fish in the cod family.

langust spiny lobster (*Palinurus vulgaris*).

lapp pancake made with cultured milk and leavening agent in the batter. Also called *svele*. A tiny version of *lapp* is called *skjebladkake*. Compare with *pannekake,* which has no cultured milk or leavening agent in the batter. Also see *Menu Guide*.

laubærblad bay leaf.

lefse traditional, soft, griddle-fried Norwegian flatbread with many regional variations. Differences include the use of various flours—rye, barley, or wheat, or a combination of the three—the addition of mashed potatoes, use of leavening agents, and spreads.

leskedrikk soft drink; also called *brus*.

lettmelk low-fat milk.

lettrømme light sour cream.

lettstekt lightly cooked.

lettøl light beer; pale ale. Also called *lyst øl*.

leverpostei liver pâté.

leverpølse liver sausage.

likør liqueur.

limabønne lima bean.

linfrø flaxseed.

linse lentil.

loff loaf of white bread.

loganbær loganberry (*Rubus loganobaccus*), a fruit generated by crossing cultivars of blackberry and raspberry. It is eaten raw or cooked.

lompe soft, flat potato pancake, typically used in place of a bun for hot dogs.

lunsje lunch.

lyr pollack (*Pollachius pollachius*), a member of the cod family.

lys light sugar syrup.

lysing European hake (*Merluccius merluccius*), a member of the cod family.

lyst øl light beer; pale ale. Also called *lettøl*.

løk onion.

løkpulver onion powder.

lønnesirup maple syrup.
lønnesukker maple sugar.
løpstikke lovage.
løvetann dandelion.
lår leg.

magerost low-fat cheese.
mais corn.
maisgryn cornmeal.
maiskolbe ear of corn.
maismel corn flour.
maisolje corn oil.
majones mayonnaise.
makrell Atlantic mackerel (*Scomber scombrus*).
maltøl malt beer.
mandel almond.
mandeldeig almond paste; also called *mandelmasse*.
mandelkremle prized variety of mushroom (*Russula integra*) with firm white flesh that tastes of almonds. See *kremle*.
mandelolje almond oil.
mangold Swiss chard; also called *bladbete*.
marengs meringue.
margarin margarine.
marinert marinated.
markjordbær wild strawberry.
mat food; another word for food is *kost*.
matbit morsel of food.
mateple cooking apple.
matfat dish for food; dish of food.
matfett lard; cooking fat.
matkarse garden cress; also called simply *karse*.
matolje cooking oil.
matvarer groceries.
medisterkaker pork patties.
medisterpølse pork sausage.
meieriprodukter dairy produce.
mel flour.

125

melbolle dumpling.

melis powdered sugar.

melisglasur icing or glaze made from powdered sugar.

melkebutikk dairy store.

melkepulver powdered milk; also called *tørrmelk*.

melkesjokolade milk chocolate.

melkesuppe milk soup.

merian marjoram.

middag dinner, the major and only hot meal of the day.

middagstallerken plate.

mineralvann mineral water, which usually is carbonated.

mjød mead.

moden ripe.

molletegg soft-boiled egg.

morbær mulberry.

morkel morel.

multe grey mullet (*Mugil capito*). *Multe* is also shorthand for *multebær*.

multebær cloudberry (*Rubus camaemorus*), a much-prized, amber-colored fruit resembling a small raspberry. Cloudberries are used to make jams, toppings, cakes, and other desserts. Also simply called *molte* or *multe*.

multesyltetøy cloudberry jam.

mungobønne mung bean.

muskat nutmeg; also called *muskatnøtt*.

muskatblomme mace.

mynte mint.

myse whey.

mysost brown cheese made from whey without the additives of milk or cream. Also called *primost*, or simply *prim*. See *brunost*.

mør tender.

mørbrad tenderloin. Also called *mørbradbiff*.

mørdeig pastry dough.

måltid meal.

måsegg seagull egg.

natron baking soda.

nedlagt canned; preserved.

nektarin nectarine.

nellik clove.

nepe turnip.
nettmelon muskmelon.
nyre kidney.
nøkkelost cheese with cloves and caraway.
nøtt nut.

oksebryst beef brisket.
oksekjøtt beef; another word for beef is *storfekjøtt*.
oksestek roast beef.
oliven olive.
olivenolje olive oil.
olje oil.
oppdrettfisk farmed fish.
oppskåret sliced.
oppskåret kjøtt cold cuts.
orrfugl black grouse (*Lyrurus tetrix*).
ost cheese.
ostehøvel cheese plane.
ostemasse curd; also called *ostestoff*.
ovnstekt oven-roasted. See *stekt*.

pai pie.
panert breaded.
pannekake crépe-like pancake. A smaller and thicker pancake made with cultured milk and a leavening agent in the batter is called *lapp* or *svele*. *Skjebladkake* is a tiny version of *lapp* or *svele*. See *Menu Guide*.
paprika bell pepper.
paranøtt Brazil nut.
pastinakk parsnip.
pattegris suckling pig.
peanøtt peanut; also called *jordnøtt*.
peanøttsmør peanut butter.
pekannøtt pecan nut.
peledsik peled, or northern whitefish (*Peled coregonus*).
pepperkake gingerbread cookie.
pepperrot horseradish.
perlegryn pearl barley.

127

perleløk pearl onion; pickling onion. Also called *sylteløk*.

perlesukker granulated sugar.

persille parsley; also called *kruspersille*.

persillerot parsley root.

piggsopp hedgehog mushroom (*Hydnum repandum*). See *blek piggsopp*.

piggvar turbot (*Psetta maxima*).

pils pilsener; light beer.

pinjekjerne pine nut.

pisket krem whipped cream; also called simply *krem*.

plantefett vegetable fat (a solid).

planteolje vegetable oil.

plomme plum.

portulakk purslane.

posjert poached. Another word for poached is *kokt*.

postei pâté; spread; meat pie.

potet potato.

potetball potato dumpling. Also called *kumle* and *raspeball*.

potetchips potato chips; also called *potetgull*.

potetmel potato flour.

prim soft cheese spread made from whey. Also called *primost* and *mysost*. See *brunost*.

pultost soft, non-fat, sour-milk cheese used as a spread.

pulverkaffe instant coffee.

purre leek. Also called *purreløk*.

pære pear.

pæresaft concentrated pear juice.

pølse sausage; hot dog. Also see *korv*.

pålegg toppings for open-face sandwiches.

rabarbra rhubarb.

rakfisk fermented freshwater fish, especially trout. Gutted fish are submerged in brine for 2–3 months at low temperature and eaten raw, traditionally sliced, on a piece of flatbread.

raps rape, or rapeseed (*Brassica napus*).

rapsolje rapeseed oil or canola oil.

raspeball potato dumpling; also called *kumle* and *potetball*.

reddik radish.

regnbueørret rainbow trout (*Salmo gairdneri*).

regningen the bill or check.

reinsdyr reindeer (*Rangifer tarandus*); also called simply *rein*. See *dyr*.

reinsdyrkjøtt reindeer meat.

reinsdyrskav shaved frozen reindeer meat. Also called *finnbiff*.

reke deep-water shrimp; northern shrimp (*Pandalus borealis*).

rett dish; course.

ribbe rib.

rips red or white currant.

ris rice.

ristede brødterninger croutons.

ristet roasted; toasted. See *stekt*.

ristet brød toast; toasted bread.

rive grate; shred; grind.

roe sugar beet; turnip.

roesukker beet sugar.

rogn fish roe.

rognebær rowanberry (*Sorbus ancuparia*). Bitter when fresh, rowanberries are made into jams and jellies, which traditionally accompany game dishes.

rom rum.

romanosalat romaine or cos lettuce; also called *bindsalat* and *romersalat*.

rosenkål Brussels sprouts.

rosévin rosé wine.

rosin raisin.

rosmarin rosemary.

rotfrukt root vegetable.

rotstappe mashed roots.

rug rye.

rugbrød rye bread.

rughvete triticale, a hybrid of wheat and rye.

rugmel rye flour.

rundstykke hard roll.

russisk stør Russian sturgeon (*Acipenser gueldenstaedtii*).

rype rock or mountain ptarmigan (*Lagopus muta*), a game bird in the grouse family. Also called *fjellrype*.

rød red.

rødbete red beet.

rødfisk ocean perch; redfish (*Sebastes marinus*). Also called *uer*.

rødkål red cabbage.

FOODS & FLAVORS GUIDE

rødløk red onion.

rødsalat radicchio.

rødspette European plaice (*Pleuronectes platessa*), a highly prized flatfish with smooth, brown skin and small, reddish-orange spots.

rødvin red wine.

rødvinseddik red wine vinegar.

rømme sour cream.

rørsukker cane sugar.

røye arctic char (*Salvelinus alpinus*), a freshwater and saltwater fish closely related to the trout and the salmon. Also called *ishhavsrøye* and *sjørøye*.

røykt smoked.

røykt fisk smoked fish.

røykt laks smoked salmon.

røykt pølse smoked sausage.

røykt sild kipper (smoked herring).

røykt skinke smoked ham.

rå raw.

rådyr roe deer. See *dyr*.

råkost uncooked fruits and vegetables.

råstekt rare, underdone (meat, for example); another word for *råstekt* is *blodig*.

råsukker unrefined sugar.

saft concentrated juice, which must be diluted before drinking. Typically, *saft* is mixed with water or soda water. Norwegians use the English word juice for juice.

salat lettuce; salad.

sallami pølse salami.

saltsild pickled herring.

salvie sage.

sanktpeterfisk John Dory (*Zeus faber*); also called St. Peter's fish.

sardin sardine or pilchard.

sau lamb or mutton. Another word for lamb or mutton is *får*. Both words refer to the animal (*sau* more so) as well as the meat. Specific words for the meat are *fårekjøtt* and *sauekjøtt*.

saus sauce; gravy. Another word for gravy is *sjysaus*.

savoykål Savoy cabbage.

sei saithe or coalfish (*Pollachius virens*), a member of the cod family.

sellerifrø celery seed.

sellerikål Chinese celery cabbage (*Brassica campestris* var. *chinensis*).

sellerirot celery root or celeriac.

semulegryn semolina.

sennep mustard.

sepia cuttlefish (*Sepiola atlantica*).

serviett napkin.

servitor waitress; waiter.

sesamfrø sesame seed.

sesamolje sesame oil.

sevruga sturgeon (*Acipenser stellatus*). Also called *stør*.

sik common whitefish (*Coregonus lavaretus*).

sikorisalat endive (not curly) or Belgian endive (*Cichorium intybus* var. *foliosum*).

sild Atlantic herring (*Clupea harengus harengus*), a somewhat larger fish than *strømming*, the Baltic herring (*Clupea harengus membras*).

sitron lemon.

sitronskall lemon zest.

sjallottløk shallot.

sjampinjong mushroom; also the name for the common button mushroom (*Agaricus bisporus*).

sjokolade chocolate.

sjy (meat) juice; au jus.

sjysaus gravy. It can also be called simply *saus*.

sjøkreps Norway lobster (*Nephrops norvegicus*), a slim, orange-colored lobster in the northeastern Atlantic. Also called *bokstavhummer*.

sjørøye arctic char (*Salvelinus alpinus*), a freshwater and saltwater fish that is closely related to the trout and the salmon. Also called *ishavsrøye* and *røye*.

sjøtunge sole (*Solea vulgaris*), a highly prized flatfish. Also called simply *tunge* and *tungeflyndre*.

sjøørret sea trout; brown trout (*Salmo trutta*).

skalldyr shellfish.

skank shank.

skinke ham.

skje spoon.

skjebladkake tiny pancake made with cultured milk and leavening agent in the batter. Larger versions are called *lapp* or *svele*. Compare with *pannekake*, which has no cultured milk or leavening agent in the batter. Also see *Menu Guide*.

skjell generic term for mussel; shellfish.

skjære cut; slice.

skorsonerrot black salsify (*Scorzonera hispanica*), a long, thin root vegetable with black skin and white flesh.

skrei spawning codfish. This term is also generally associated with the arctic cod species (*Arctogadus glacialis*). Also see *torsk*.

skrell peelings; rinds.

skrubbe European flounder (*Platichthys flesus*).

skummetmelk skim milk.

skål bowl; saucer.

slettvar brill (*Rhombus laevis*), a flatfish closely related to the turbot.

slåpebær sloeberry (*Prunus spinosa*), a small, tart, dark-blue berry in the plum family, which is used to make preserves.

smelteost processed cheese.

smult lard.

smultring doughnut.

smør butter.

smørbrød open-face sandwich.

smørdeig puff pastry; also called *butterdeig*.

smørvalnøtt butternut or white walnut (*Juglans cinerea*).

småkake cookie. Other words for cookie are *kake* and *kjeks*.

snegl snail.

snittebønne string bean.

sodavann soda water.

sodd broth; soup-like dish with vegetables and meat cooked separately.

solbær black currant.

solsikkefrø sunflower seed.

solsikkeolje sunflower oil.

sopp mushroom.

soppsaus mushroom sauce or gravy.

soyabønne soybean.

soyaolje soybean oil.

speilegg fried egg.

speke cure.

spekeflesk cured (salted and dried) bacon.

spekekjøtt cured (salted and dried) meat.

spekemat cured (salted and dried) meat or fish.

spekepølse hard smoked sausage.

spekesild herring preserved in salt.

spekeskinke cured (salted and dried) ham.

spinat spinach.

spiseeple eating apple; also called *søteple*. The general term for apple is *eple*.

spisekart menu.

spisskarve cumin; also simply called *karve*.

sprettmais popcorn.

sprit alcohol; spirits.

sprø crisp.

steinbit catfish. Two species of arctic catfish are enjoyed in Norway for their firm, tasty white flesh: the spotted catfish (*Anarhichas minor*) and Atlantic catfish (*Anarhichas lupus*). The Atlantic catfish is more abundant and not as prized as the spotted catfish. Another common name for these fish is wolffish. They are dissimilar in taste to the channel catfish (*Ictalurus punctatus*) found in the United States, which is now mostly farmed.

steinsopp porcini mushroom (*Boletus edulis*).

stek roast (cut of meat).

stekt general word indicating food has been cooked in one of three different ways: fried, roasted, or braised. A more specific word for braised is *gryteskekt*. More specific words for roasted are *ristet* (meaning something dry such as bread is roasted or toasted) and *helstekt* (meaning something wet such as meat is roasted). Also see *ovnstekt*.

sterkvin fortified wine; also called *hetvin*.

stikkelsbær gooseberry.

stikkelsbærsyltetøy gooseberry jam.

stjerneanis star anise (*Illicium verum*).

stokkfisk "stockfish," unsalted, air-dried fish, especially cod. After the heads are removed, the fish are gutted, tied together in pairs by the tail, and hung over poles, or sticks (*stokker*), to dry. Fish similarly prepared and hung on large wooden racks (*hjeller*) to dry are called *tørrfisk*, but the fish product is the same as *stokkfisk*. See *tørrfisk*. Also see *klippfisk*.

stor gaffel table fork.

stor kniv table knife.

storfekjøtt beef. Another word for beef is *oksekjøtt*.

stort kamskjell king scallop, great scallop, or Saint-Jacques scallop (*Pecten maximus*). Also called simply *kamskjell*.

strandkrabbe common shore crab or green crab (*Carcinus maenas*).

strømming Baltic herring (*Clupea harengus membras*), a variety of herring in the Baltic sea. *Strømming* are somewhat smaller than *sild,* the Atlantic herring (*Clupea harengus harengus*). Baltic herring are also called *østersjøsild*.

stuet creamed.

stør sturgeon (*Acipenser stellatus*). Also called *sevruga*.

sukker sugar.

sukkerert sugar snap pea.

sukkernepe rutabaga; swede (*Brassica napus* var. *napobrassica*). Other names for rutabaga are *kålrabi* and *kålrot*. Note that the kohlrabi (*Brassica oleracea* var. *gongylodes*) is not called *kålrabi* but *knutekål* in Norwegian.

sukkertøy sweets; candies. Also called *gotteri*.

suppeskje soup spoon.

sur sour; pickled.

surbrød sourdough bread.

surkål sauerkraut.

surmelk curdled milk; sour milk. Also called *tykkmelk*.

surost sour-milk cheese; cottage cheese.

sursild pickled herring.

svart bringebær black raspberry.

svart kaffe black coffee.

svart pepper black pepper.

svart valnøtt black walnut.

sveitserost Swiss cheese.

svele pancake made with cultured milk and leavening agent in the batter. Also called *lapp*. A tiny version of *svele* is called *skjebladkake*. Compare with *pannekake*, which has no cultured milk or leavening agent in the batter. Also see *Menu Guide*.

sverdfisk swordfish (*Xiphias gladius*).

svin pig; also called *gris*, which also refers to pork.

svinekjøtt pork; other words for pork are *gris* and *grisekjøtt*. Also see *flesk*.

sviske prune.

sylte pickle. Refers to both the food item preserved and the process used to preserve it.

sylteløk pearl onion; pickling onion. Also called *perleløk*.

syltetøy jam; jelly. May also refer to aspic.

sørhare hare; also called simply *hare*.

søt sweet.

søt vin sweet wine; dessert wine.

søteple eating apple. Also called *spiseeple*. The general term for apple is *eple*.

søtpotet sweet potato.

tallerken plate.

tang kelp; seaweed.

tangbrosme fourbeard rockling (*Enchelyopus cimbrius*), a fish in the cod family. Also called *firetrådet*.

terte torte.

tettemelk curdled milk; cultured milk.

timian thyme.

tindved small orange berries from the sea buckthorn shrub (*Hippophae rhamnoides*), used to make pies and jams.

torsk cod. The species inhabiting the coastal waters (*Gadus morhua*) does not migrate to any great extent, whereas the arctic cod (*Arctogadus glacialis*) is found mainly in off-shore waters. Also see *skrei*.

torskekinn cod cheek.

torsketunge cod "tongue," a triangular muscle in the floor of the mouth.

traktkantarell funnel-shaped chanterelle mushroom (*Cantharellus tubaeformis*).

tranebær cranberry.

tunfisk tuna.

tunge tongue. Also the name for sole (*Solea vulgaris*); see *sjøtunge*. Sole is also called *tungeflyndre*.

tykkmelk curdled milk; sour milk. Also called *surmelk*.

tyttebær lingonberry or whortleberry (*Vaccinium vitis-idaea*). The berries are sweetened and eaten as jams or juice, typically with game meats.

tørr dry.

tørrfisk unsalted, air-dried fish, especially cod. Pairs of gutted fish with heads removed are typically tied together by the tail and hung on large wooden racks (*hjeller*) to dry. Unsalted fish similarly processed but hung over poles or sticks (*stokker*) are called *stokkfisk,* but the product is the same as *tørrfisk*. The preservation process of air drying unsalted fish predates that of air drying salted fish (see *klippfisk*).

tørrmelk powdered milk; also called *melkepulver*.

uer redfish; ocean perch (*Sebastes marinus*). Also called *rødfisk*.

umoden unripe; green.

urtete herbal tea.

uten kolsyre still (not carbonated).

vaktel quail (*Coturnix coturnix*).

valmuefrø poppy seed.

valnøtt walnut.

valnøttolje walnut oil.

vann water.

vannmelon watermelon.

varme pølse hot dog. Also called *wienerpølse*.

varme sjokolade hot chocolate, cocoa.

vegetarianer vegetarian; also called *vegetarisk*.

velling gruel; thin cooked cereal.

villkanin wild rabbit.

vilt game animal.

vin wine.

vindrue grape.

vineddik vinegar.

vinkart wine list.

vintergrønn wintergreen or teaberry. Also called *krypberglyng*.

voksbønne wax bean.

vørterøl non-alcoholic beer made from water, malt, and hops.

vågehval minke whale.

vårløk spring onion or scallion.

wienerpølse hot dog. Also called simply *pølse*. Another name for hot dog is *varme pølse*.

øl beer; ale.

ørret trout (*Salmo trutta*).

ørretabbor black bass; largemouth black bass (*Micropterus salmoides*). Also called *laksabbor*.

østers common oyster (*Ostrea edulis*).

østersjøsild Baltic herring (*Clupea harengus membras*). Also called *strømming*.

åkerbær arctic raspberry or arctic bramble (*Rubus arcticus*), a dark-red fruit that looks like a dwarf raspberry. This sweet, juicy berry grows in northern Norway and is used for jams, liqueurs, and flavoring tea.

ål eel.

Food Establishments

A Quick Reference Guide to Restaurants Visited

The following food establishments were visited while in Norway researching *Eat Smart in Norway*. Most provided cooking demonstrations. The chefs at these establishments are listed in the *Acknowledgements* (p. xi). Some of the recipes they provided appear in *Tastes of Norway,* p. 45.

The telephone country code for Norway is 47. (You must first dial 011 from the US for international calls.)

Restaurants

Bryggen Tracteursted Bryggestredet 2, N-5003 Bergen
Tel (47) (0) 55 31 40 46   www.bryggentracteur.no
booking@bellevue.no

Byrkjedalstunet Byrkjedal, 4335 Dirdal
Tel (47) (0) 51 61 29 00   www.byrkjedalstunet.no
post@btunet.no

Enhjorningen Enhjørningsgården 29, 5003 Bergen
Tel (47) (0) 55 30 69 50   www.enhjorningen.no
info@enhjorningen.no

Fleischer's Hotel Evangervegen 13, N-5700 Voss
Tel (47) (0) 56 52 05 00   www.fleischers.no
hotel@fleischers.no

Fossheim Hotell 2688 Lom
Tel (47) (0) 61 21 95 00   www.fossheimhotel.no
resepsjon@fossheimhotel.no

Fretheim Hotel PB 63, 5743 Flåm
Tel (47) (0) 57 63 63 00   www.fretheim-hotel.no
mail@fretheim-hotel.no

Frognerseteren Holmenkollveien 200, N-0791 Oslo
Tel (47) (0) 22 92 40 40   www.frognerseteren.no
booking@frognerseteren.no
Hanne på Høyden Fosswinckelsgate 18, 5007 Bergen
Tel (47) (0) 55 32 34 32   www.spisestedet.no
post@spisestedet.no
Petrines Gjestgiveri AS N-6214 Norddal
Tel (47) (0) 70 25 92 85   www.petrines.com
petrines@online.no
Rica Nidelven Hotel Havnegata 1-3, N-7400 Trondheim
Tel (47) (0) 73 56 80 00   www.ricanidelven.no
rica.nidelven.hotel@rica.no
Røros Hotell N-7374 Røros
Tel (47) (0) 72 40 80 00   www.roroshotell.no
post@roroshotell.no
Sans og Samling Lian Lian Road 36, 7025 Trondheim
Tel (47) (0) 72 56 51 10   www.sansogsamling.no
kontakt@lianrestaurant.no
Sjohuset Skagen Skagenkaien 16, 4006 Stavanger
Tel (47) (0) 51 89 51 80   www.sjohusetskagen.no
post@sjohusetskagen.no
Spa-Hotell Velvære Hjelmeland 4130 Hjelmeland
Tel (47) (0) 48 05 06 00   www.spahotellvelvare.no
post@spahotellvelvaere.no
To Rom og Kjøkken Carl Johans gate 5, 7010 Trondheim
Tel (47) (0) 73 56 89 00   www.toromogkjokken.no
post@2rok.no
Tuddal Høyfjellshotel N-3697, Tuddal
Tel (47) (0) 35 02 88 88   www.tuddal.no
gurholt@tuddal.no

Bibliography

Almås, Reidar, editor. *Norwegian Agricultural History*. Trondheim, Norway: Tapir Academic Press, 2004.

Andersson, Espen Bowitz, editor. *Bryggen: The Hanseatic Settlement in Bergen*. Bergen, Norway: Det Hanseatiske Museum, 1982.

Brimi, Arne and Ardis Kaspersen. *Norwegian National Recipes: An inspiring journey in the culinary history of Norway*. Lisa Gay Bostwick, trans. Pullman, Washington: Skaldaspillar Publications, 2000.

Chartrand, R., K. Durham, M. Harrison, and I. Heath. *The Vikings: Voyagers of Discovery and Plunder*. Oxford: Osprey Publishing, 2006.

Daniels, H.K. *Home Life in Norway*. New York: The MacMillan Company, 1911.

Daub, Siri Lise. *Tastes & Tales of Norway*. New York: Hippocrene Books, Inc., 2002.

Graham-Campbell, James and Dafydd Kidd. *The Vikings*. London: British Museum Publications Ltd, 1980.

Hagen, Anders. *Norway: Ancient Peoples and Places*. New York: Frederick A. Praeger, Inc., 1967.

Helle, Knut, editor. *The Cambridge History of Scandinavia. Volume 1. Prehistory to 1520*. Cambridge: Cambridge University Press, 2003.

Henry, Bernard. *Vikings and Norsemen*. London: John Baker Publishers, 1971.

Herteig, Asbjørn, Hans-Emil Lidén, and Charlotte Blinheim. *Archaeological contributions to the early history of urban communities in Norway*. Oslo: Universitetsforlaget, 1975.

Hjelle, Kari Loe. Foreign trade and local production: plant remains from medieval times in Norway. In *Medieval Food Traditions in Northern Europe*, edited by Sabine Karg. Publications from the National Museum, Studies in Archaeology & History, Vol. 12. Copenhagen, Denmark: The National Museum of Denmark, 2007.

Hovig, Ingrid Espelid. *The Best of Norwegian Traditional Cuisine*. Mary Lee Nielsen, trans. Oslo: Gyldendal Norsk Forlag, 1992.

Hovig, Ingrid Espelid. *Julemat*. Oslo: Gyldendal Norsk Forlag ASA, 1997.

BIBLIOGRAPHY

Jesch, Judith. *Women in the Viking Age*. Woodbridge, Suffolk, United Kingdom: The Boydell Press, 2003.

Kurlansky, Mark. *The Basque History of the World*. New York: Penguin Books, 2001.

Kurlansky, Mark. *Cod: A Biography of the Fish that Changed the World*. New York: Penguin Books, 1998.

Kurlansky, Mark. *Salt: A World History*. New York: Penguin Books, 2002.

Larsen, Karen. *A History of Norway*. Princeton, New Jersey: Princeton University Press, 1950.

Laurence, Janet. *The Food & Cooking of Norway*. London: Aquamarine, 2007.

Libæk, Ivar and Øivind Stenersen. *A History of Norway from the Ice Age to the Age of Petroleum*, 2nd edition. Jean Aase, trans. Oslo: Grøndahl og Dreyers Forlag AS, 1995.

Lødøen, Trond and Gro Mandt. *The Rock Art of Norway*. Oxford: Windgather Press, 2010.

Magnus, Olaus. *Description of the Northern Peoples. Rome 1555*. (Peter Fisher and Humphrey Higgens, trans.). London: The Hakluyt Society, 1998.

Moen, Frank Emil. *Marine Fish & Invertebrates of Northern Europe*. Sabine Cochrane and Fredrik Pleijel, trans. Essex: AquaPress, 2004.

Notaker, Henry. Between innovation and tradition. In *Culinary cultures of Europe: Identity, diversity and dialogue,* edited by Darra Goldstein and Kathrin Merkle, pp. 319–331. Strasbourg, France: Council of Europe Publishing, 2005.

Notaker, Henry. *Food Culture in Scandinavia*. Westport, Connecticut: Greenwood Press, 2009.

Notaker, Henry. A thousand years of Norwegian food. In *This Is Norway,* edited by Arne Bonde, pp. 176–197. Oslo: J.M. Stenersens Forlag A.S., 1992.

Riddervold, Astri. *Lutefisk, Rakefisk and Herring in Norwegian Tradition*. Oslo: Novus Press, 1990.

Schildhauer, Johannes. *The Hansa: History and Culture*. Katherine Vanovitch, trans. Leipzig, Germany: Druckerei Fortschritt Erfurt, 1985.

Shetelig, Haakon and Hjalmar Falk. *Scandinavian Archaeology*. Oxford: Oxford University Press, 1937.

Wheeler, Sara. *The Magnetic North: Notes from the Arctic Circle*. New York: Farrar, Straus and Giroux, 2009.

Wolf, Kirsten. *The Daily Life of the Vikings*. Westport, Connecticut: Greenwood Press, 2004.

Urba czyk, Przemysław. *Medieval Arctic Norway*. Warsaw, Poland: Semper, 1992.

Øye, Ingvild, editor. *Bergen and the German Hansa*. Bergen, Norway: Bryggens Museum, 1994.

Index

design   Ekeby
cover design   Susan P. Chwae
color printing   Traver Graphics, Inc.
book production   Sheridan Books, Inc.

typefaces   Garamond Simoncini and Helvetica Black
paper   60# Offset